The Tears of God

Jesus as Passion and Promise

Lent and Easter
Cycle C Sermons
based on the Gospel Texts

Susan R. Andrews

CSS Publishing Company, Inc.
Lima, Ohio

THE TEARS OF GOD

FIRST EDITION

Library of Congress Cataloging-in-Publication Data

Andrews, Susan R., 1949-
The tears of God : Jesus as passion and promise : Lent and Easter, Cycle C sermons based on the Gospel texts / Susan R. Andrews. -- 1st ed.
p. cm.
ISBN 0-7880-2683-6 (alk. paper)
1. Lenten sermons. 2. Easter--Sermons. 3. Bible. N.T. Gospels--Sermons. 4. Lectionary preaching. 5. Common lectionary (1992). Year C. I. Title.
BV4277.A53 2012
252'.62--dc23

2012009967

For more information about CSS Publishing Company resources, visit our website at www.csspub.com, email us at csr@csspub.com, or call (800) 241-4056.

ISBN-13: 978-0-7880-2683-6
ISBN-10: 0-7880-2683-6

PRINTED IN USA

This book is dedicated
to Sim —
compass and companion
for forty years

Table of Contents

Preface

Preaching is a privilege. To dare to proclaim the living word of God is to engage in the mysterious work of incarnation. And so, preaching takes both courage and humility. Nothing trivializes God more than a sloppy sermon or a lazy preacher. Our people are starving for a nourishing word, and we dare not feed them junk food.

After 38 years as a pastor and spiritual leader, I still tremble every time I step into a pulpit. Yes, I still use pulpits and manuscripts. For me, creating a sermon is like painting a picture — each word, phrase, and image becomes part of a larger canvas. Writing and re-writing a sermon brings me deep pleasure, and it invites me to fall more deeply in love with God.

At its best, a sermon puts flesh on the bones of a biblical text — allowing the printed word to jump off the page into the lives of the listeners. Therefore, knowing the listeners is essential preparation work for any sermon. Since the word is alive in the living Christ, any particular sermon needs to speak to a particular people in a particular place at a particular time. It doesn't hurt to make sure each sermon is in dialogue with contemporary culture — sensitive to the language of blogs and YouTube clips and front page headlines. I have taken Karl Barth's advice to heart. I always create a sermon with the Bible in one hand and the newspaper in the other.

The strongest sermons are those that are part of a three-way conversation — among the preacher, the congregation, and God. It is the stories, hungers, and questions of the congregation that instruct a preacher over the years, and so the narrative of scripture becomes the narrative of the congregation. I am deeply indebted to the people of Bradley Hills Presbyterian Church in Bethesda, Maryland, where many of these sermons were preached. They loved me, prodded me, and changed me during our seventeen years of traveling together, and they shaped me into the preacher and the pastor I am today.

The season of Lent has always been the center point of my own spiritual journey. The rich shadows, the deep stories, the shattered serenity of the biblical texts snatch us from the platitudes and pleasantries of shallow living and drag us into the very presence of God.

C.S. Lewis famously describes Jesus as the "tears of God." As we traverse the rugged terrain of Lent and Eastertide, may we discover that those tears soften our sorrow and nurture our joy. My prayer is that these sermons will bless you as they have blessed me — with the passion and the promise of Jesus — the word who continues to become flesh in the daily-ness of our living.

— Susan R. Andrews

Ash Wednesday
Matthew 6:1-6, 16-21

Journey Toward Humility

Unto the mercy of Almighty God,
We commend the soul of our brother departed,
and we commit his body to the ground,
earth to earth,
ashes to ashes,
dust to dust,
in sure and certain hope
of the resurrection to eternal life,
through Jesus Christ our Lord.
— PCUSA Book of Common Worship

I remember that I was afraid to touch the ashes. There they were, about five pounds of fine grey matter, with bits of white bone scattered throughout. We had picked them up at the funeral home, and then Mary held Greg in her lap as we drove back to Mill Run. Now it was time. We were gathered on the bridge overlooking McClure Creek and all the nieces and nephews were nervously running around. My husband opened the box and unfastened the plastic bag inside. For a moment, time stopped. How could it be? How could 44 years of elegance, energy, joy, sorrow, beauty, strength, pain — how could it be contained in that one small box? We all tentatively reached out and touched mortality. And then the children took fistfuls of ash, and let them fly — arcing over the bridge — into the water. There went Gregory. He was passing from death back into life and into the gracious and eternal arms of God. He, who had been killed by the cruelty of AIDS, he who had been judged by the cruelty of society, he who had been punished by the cruelty of his own guilt — there he was — floating, from the creek into the river, from the river into the sea — into the sea of God's infinite grace and mercy. My brother-in-law was finally free.

In the ancient wisdom of the church, each Ash Wednesday we touch each other with the ashes of our mortality. As we enter the desert struggle of Lent, we are invited to acknowledge our finitude, to offer our incompleteness, to embrace our total dependence on the wholeness and health of God. As the ashes smear our forehead, the traditional words of blessing are offered:

Remember that you are dust,
and to dust you shall return.

It is in the brutal honesty of this ritual that we tell the truth about who we are. We are ushered into the barren truth of the Lenten wilderness.

At the heart of any Lenten discipline is humility. This word is connected to the Latin *humus* — the word for earth. In Genesis we are told that God took simple earth and blew breath into it to create Adam — *adam* — the word for humanity. Indeed, we are dust and we know that it is to dust — to earth — to *humus* that we return. How can we be anything but humble?

Now let us be clear. Humility and humiliation are two very different things. Rather than diminishing the fullness of our lives, humility fills us back up. Humility demands time and humility invites courage and discipline — the ability to get out of the way, so that God can move in.

Our Matthew text for this evening paints a picture of humility. On this canvas, we do not disappear. Instead, God has plenty of room to appear, flourishing in the desert of our dreams. Rather than pompous piety, we are called to quiet joy. Rather than breast-beating ostentation, we are called to deep and daily devotion. The purpose of our sojourn with humility is not so we can earn God's approval, but so God can woo our hearts.

The older I get, the more I yearn for the desert places of Lent; for long quiet days; for dark, somber music; and for honest earthy stories of finitude and failure. Not because I am depressed but because I long to hear the truth — the truth about sin and brokenness, death and despair — the truth about the shadow side of living. During Lent, my self-delusions crumble, my masks of pretense come off, and I find fresh courage to look into the mirror of my imperfection. It is enormously liberating. Because it is there — in the glare of the truth — that I most experience the grace, tenderness, and touch of God. It is there I discover how utterly dependent I am upon our utterly dependable God. It is there I finally feel safe.

The story is told of a traveler who was lost in the desert. As he wandered for days, he became more parched and disoriented. Up hills and down hills and through the bitter night and the blistering day, he searched for water. But he found nothing. Finally he stumbled and fell and found no more energy to get up and try again. He lost all hope of survival.

It was only then that he began to pay attention to the utter silence around him — to the sound of total silence in the desert. With consciousness fading away, he suddenly heard something — a sound so faint that only sheer silence could detect it. It was the sound of running water. Revived by hope, the traveler dragged his body toward the sound and soon immersed himself in a pool of fresh, cool water.

What is it this Lenten season that is obscuring the sounds, the tastes, the promises of God? What is the cacophony of worries, pressures, and obsessions keeping us from slowing down and opening up and hearing the sweet silence of God? In what ways are we so puffed up in body, mind, and spirit that we find it impossible to lie prostrate before the presence of God? Why is it we prefer the distraction of television and Facebook and shopping malls to the quiet rhythms of a Lenten discipline? Why do we keep racing to do more, and have more, and be more, rather than savoring the fleeting fragility of life? Why is it so few of us have the courage to gather in the shadows of this night to receive the barren blessing of ashes?

Every day I wear a simple silver bracelet on my wrist. It used to belong to Arabella but now it is mine. Years ago, Arabella was fierce and faithful and full of life. Four years ago, Arabella was diagnosed with pancreatic cancer. Two years ago, Arabella died, vanquished by the violence of a vicious disease. All that is left are her ashes, cradled in a wooden box. *Remember that you are dust, and to dust you shall return.*

The two years between diagnosis and death were, for Arabella, a vast and barren desert. She was wandering, struggling, and hoping against hope that she would find a stream of healing. Along the way she discovered rich companions in the desert — a devoted husband who wandered with her, friends who helped her laugh and family who re-told her story. She developed a discipline of quiet, prayer, writing, painting, and reflecting that deepened her pool of gratitude and joy for the gift of her sixty years of living. There finally came the time when her body crumbled, and she found little energy to keep wandering. It was then she heard most clearly the sound of God's sheer silence, calling her home. Arabella hated dying, but she never hated living. She was ready to live again — in the time and place of God's great mystery.

Psalm 116 — picked out by Arabella in the final months of her life — formed the fertile soil for her Service of Witness to the Resurrection. Though her body had returned to dust, her soul sang forth from the words of the psalmist: humble words of a humble servant — still feisty and faithful and full of life:

What shall I return to the Lord for all his bounty to me?
I will lift up the cup of salvation
and call upon the name of the Lord,
I will pay my vows to the Lord
in the presence of all his people.
Precious in the sight of the Lord
is the death of his faithful ones.
O Lord, I am your servant;
I am your servant, the child of your serving girl.
You have loosed my bonds.
I will offer to you a thanksgiving sacrifice
and call on the name of the Lord.
I will pay my vows to the Lord
in the presence of all his people,
in the courts of the house of the Lord,
in your midst, O Jerusalem.
Praise the Lord!

People of God, this night we are being called to a discipline of humility, a journey of wandering, a blessing of mortality — trusting that God will meet us in the shadows and feed us in the barren places. Be bold to receive the blessing of these ashes and rejoice in God's promise of finitude, fragility, and eternal life.

May it be so. Amen.

Lent 1
Luke 4:1-13

Welcome to the Wilderness

A friend of mine tells the story of his youngest daughter's baptism. After the sacrament, his older daughter, who was four, was cradling her sister in her arms. She looked up and said, "Daddy, Meggy is really wet!"

This morning's story is really about baptism — about what happens after the water on our head has dried. Right after Jesus is baptized in the River Jordan, right after God has publicly chosen and named Jesus as God's very own, it is then that the Spirit — God! — leads Jesus into the barren, rocky wilderness of central Palestine. Yes, God has chosen Jesus. The question now is: Will Jesus choose God?

The season of Lent is modeled after those forty days that Jesus roamed the desert. Those forty days of hunger and thirst, of temptation and testing, of self-examination and brutal honesty. The question for us during Lent is the same. We know that through our baptism God has chosen us. How faithfully, enthusiastically, and completely are we willing to choose God?

The wilderness, Jesus' wilderness in Palestine, and our wilderness in Lent, is not about escape. It is not about turning inward and forsaking the world. It is not about claiming inward spirituality at the expense of outward discipleship. No, this wrestling and questioning, praying and fasting in the desert is about preparation for ministry. It is about moving away, for a time, from the stress and busyness, noise and distraction in order to face our fragile humanity. Yes, to face the fears, the anxieties, the self-absorption, the idolatries that stand in the way of serving God with all our heart and all our soul, with all our mind and all our strength. The wilderness is not about facing the evil that is out there. It is about facing the evil in here — about facing the evil inside our own souls. It is about owning, confessing, and acknowledging how much we run away from God's terrifying grace and demanding love. It is about how much we avoid admitting who we really are and what it is we really need.

A church in Oregon has a Laotian sexton who has turned out to be a strength and asset to the congregation. Resettled as a refugee during the post-Vietnam War years, he and his family have worked hard and become proud and accomplished United States citizens. Just a year ago, they realized a major dream by financing and building their own home. Shortly thereafter, the pastor began to notice that his colleague, the sexton, was acting anxious and preoccupied most of the time. In fact, he had developed a noticeable nervous tic in his eye. One day the sexton and the pastor had a conversation about what was going on. Apparently the sexton and his wife had been terrified ever since they moved into their new house. They had had dreams about demons haunting their home. Though they had become baptized Christians, the images and stories of their former animist religion and ancestor worship were still very much a part of their world.

Finally, one day, they asked their pastor if he would come and bless their new home, performing an exorcism of the evil spirits. Not quite sure what he was getting into, the pastor arrived only to find forty guests waiting for him. He went from room to room, with a Bible open in one hand, touching all four walls with the cross in his other hand, and saying, "I claim this room in the name of Jesus Christ who is Lord over all spirits." He went through the family room, the kitchen, the living room, and the bedrooms. He started to walk past the bathroom only to be gently pushed by his hosts onto the ceramic floor. Yes, the bathroom was blessed too! What followed next was a joyful celebration and the appreciation of two parishioners who now felt released from the evil spirits in their home (story from Rob Elder).

This may seem like an odd story to some of us, but who are we to judge the culture, the psyche, the spiritual disciplines of other people? Who are we to proclaim that the powers of evil are only the figment of some people's imaginations? Many commentators have suggested that this forty-day retreat of Jesus was an inward journey, a wrestling with the demons of his own dreams or perhaps hallucinations arising from his six-week fast. But such an interpretation in no way lessens the importance of the story. Jesus is face-to-face with the power of evil — the seductive temptation to glorify himself, to bask in the adulation of the crowds, to obey not the God who created him, but instead chose to obey the demands of his own self.

Actually when we think about it, Jesus ended up doing all those things that the devil invited him to do. He *did* feed five thousand people with wonder bread. He *did* perform spectacular miracles that wowed the crowds. He *did* end up wearing a crown of power — but not anything like the kind of power the devil had in mind. All these things Jesus did, but they happened when God wanted them to and not when Jesus wanted them to happen. They happened for the up-building of God's people and not for the up-building of Jesus' ego.

In his book, *Engaging the Powers*, Walter Wink writes about the powers and principalities, the subtle and not-so-subtle forces of evil that permeate our individual and corporate lives. What is it that shackles us to the safety of the past and inhibits our growth into God's faithful and energized people? What is it that stifles compassion and prevents civility and thwarts justice in our world? How is it that our love of self so consumes us that we turn a cold shoulder to the needs of those around us? The devil, with his seductive flattery and spectacular promises, represents all that woos us toward immediate gratification, promises resurrection without crucifixion and splashes phony rainbows in a sky that has not yet seen rain. Wink suggests that we all have a choice when it comes to these powers of evil. We can ignore them. We can placate them. Or we can engage them — wrestling with them until truth prevails.

The question we need to ask is this: Do the powers of evil in our community, in our families, in our places of work know our names? Are we sufficiently engaged in a wrestling match with those forces that are in opposition to God so that they know us and react by seducing us and tempting us and testing us in the wilderness? Or do we avoid the desert, avoid the struggle, avoid engaging those forces that deny God's sovereignty in the world? After forty days of struggle, Jesus was able to overcome the powers of evil. Why? Because he engaged them in the first place and because he remained true to his vocation as God's child. Jesus' values were self-contained and not dependent on the whims of the world. Jesus trusted that the grace of God was there to sustain him. Jesus remained true to God's values, God's heart, and God's justice. Yes, because Jesus was faithful, the power of God overcame the power of evil.

Immediately following this struggle in the wilderness, the text tells us that Jesus — still filled with the Holy Spirit — began his teaching and preaching ministry in Galilee. Not only did God lead him into the wilderness. Not only did God sustain him in the wilderness. But God re-energized him and sent him into holy ministry in the midst of an unholy world.

Years ago when I was in college, I entered a wilderness of my own. My life was falling apart around me. My sister was being abused in a violent marriage. My father was being attacked in the congregation he was serving. My first love had just dumped me with no warning and no reason given. I didn't have a clue what I was supposed to do with the rest of my life. So I crawled into the desert — onto my bed, under my quilt with all the shades drawn for several long and barren days. I wrestled with the temptations of the devil to wrap myself in self-pity, to punish everyone by contemplating suicide, to slide into the comforting womb of deep depression. My friends tried to reach out to me, but I kept the door locked. I refused to eat. I refused to talk. I refused to move off my bed. Then the Spirit of God intervened. The phone rang. It was the college chaplain, the only person in the world whom I trusted and the only person in the world whom I sensed loved me for who I really was. On some pretext he got me to come see him where he gently confronted me with my unhealthy behavior and led me to the help I needed in order to reenter the land of the living.

In retrospect, I know the desert, the wilderness under my quilt, was a place of testing and preparation for me. It was during those dark hours I realized that I needed a career, to go to graduate school, to take responsibility for my own life and to stop waiting for other people to define me. Later it was through the careful mentoring of the chaplain that I first heard the call to ministry.

When all is said and done, the wilderness — even with all its trials and temptations — can be an oasis of grace. Despite the lonesome valleys and the forbidding peaks, despite the fears and anxieties, despite the confusion and the hunger, God leads us into the wilderness for a purpose: to refine us by fire and to confront us with the most important decision of our lives. Whom shall we serve? Shall we serve the world or, living out our baptismal promises, shall we serve the one who has given us life? Once again, this Lenten season, the choice is before us. Whom shall we serve? Let us follow the Spirit into the wilderness and trust that God *will* be there to minister to us.

May it be so for you and for me. Amen.

Lent 2
Luke 13:31-35

The Holy Must

Ed Friedman was the founding rabbi of a Jewish congregation that shares sacred space with Bradley Hills Presbyterian Church in Bethesda, Maryland. He went on from there to become an accomplished family therapist and nationally known author. A few years before his death, Friedman wrote a book called *Friedman's Fables* where he presents some pithy, pushy stories that invite us into psychological and spiritual health. One of the fables is titled "The Bridge."

At the beginning we are introduced to a man who has begun a new journey at midlife — this time with great passion and the hope that he is traveling toward the true purpose of his life. Finally, he thinks, my life is beginning to make sense and I can make a difference in the world. Just as he begins to gain momentum on his journey, he runs into a stranger coming straight toward him across a bridge. The stranger has a rope tied around his waist, and when he meets our focused friend, he asks him to stop and to take hold of the end of the rope. A bit taken aback, our friend complies, and before he knows what is happening, the stranger jumps off the bridge. Now the man is dangling dangerously between bridge and water. Crying out from the end of the rope, the stranger begs the man at the top to hold onto him, for the stranger's life is now totally in his hands.

Obviously, the man at the top of the rope has a choice. He can keep moving toward his long-sought purpose. Or he can stop and save someone else's life. Then another thought occurs to him. The man at the end of the rope is not helpless. He can take responsibility for his own life by wrapping the rope around his waist several times and pulling himself up as long as the man at the top holds the rope steady. And so the man holding the rope offers the stranger in danger his own choice. The two men can become partners in salvation, or the man dangling from the rope can continue to abdicate responsibility for his own living.

When the man at the end of the rope is given the choice to participate in his own salvation — or not — he screams in panic and horror. He insists that only the man on the bridge has the responsibility of saving his life. The traveler must haul the stranger to safety.

In response, the man holding the rope accepts the other's decision. He lets go of the rope causing the fall of the troubled stranger. Then our midlife wanderer continues his journey toward the purpose of his life (Edwin Freidman, *Friedman's Fables* [The Guilford Press, 1990], pp. 12-13).

When I first read this story, I was, quite frankly, horrified. There is no way that I — or any self-respecting person — could let go of that rope. What could Friedman have been thinking of? Our tough-love, me-first world has gone too far if this cold-hearted story is seen as healthy. So in my own somewhat prejudicial way, I decided that this particular fable must be "Jewish" and that a "Christian" answer would be very different. That is until I read and really studied our gospel lesson for today.

These four short verses from Luke are packed with emotion and imagery, and they come at a crucial point in Jesus' journey. In Matthew this lament over Jerusalem occurs during Holy Week — after Palm Sunday and before Maundy Thursday when the die is already cast and Jesus is all but dead. Not so in Luke. This gospel writer describes the scene much earlier in the story, in the middle of the book, when Jesus is on his way to Jerusalem. In fact, the whole gospel of Luke takes place "on the way" to Jerusalem — on the way to this holiest of cities where God is adored in the temple

— this holiest of cities where prophets are stoned again and again for speaking the audacious truth, the truth about the cost and the gift of God's love. Ninety times Luke mentions Jerusalem — twice as many times as the rest of the New Testament combined. Jerusalem is very important to Luke. Jerusalem is very important to Jesus. So important that he weeps and laments when he senses the foolishness, the impotence, and the self-destructiveness of Jerusalem's people.

There is one particular word that jumps out of this account this morning — a word that appears again and again in Luke's intense narrative. The word is must. Jesus *must* be on his way. He *must* go to Jerusalem, he *must* go to the temple, he *must* go to Gethsemane, he *must* go to Calvary. This mission is not negotiable, it is not tentative, it is not changeable depending on how he feels. There is a passion burning in Jesus' soul, a mission, a call, a vocation that defines the very heart of who he is. And nothing and nobody can dissuade him — not crafty, foxy Herod; not the curious Pharisees; not even the hurting, scared, needy people hanging off the edges of Jerusalem — those strangers trying to stop Jesus, begging him to save them, to fix them, to heal them.

Today, the Bible is asking each of us a question: Do you have a *must*? Is there a burning passion, vision, or mission in your life that propels you, energizes you, calls you and gives you purpose, value, and strength? Some of the greatest leaders in history have shared Jesus' single-minded sense of *must* — Martin Luther King Jr. with his dream, FDR with his New Deal, Nelson Mandela with his thirty-year vision of a free South Africa. Most of us won't come anywhere near embodying such lofty and powerful ideals. But that does not let us off the hook and that should not keep us from discerning and discovering the meaningful *musts* in our own living.

What is it that motivates you, for which you are willing to take risks? What is it that can open you to failure, invites you to push your comfort zones, to maybe disappoint some people along the way? Is it the love of a child so fierce that you can withstand fear, mistakes, and struggle? Is it a vision for the church that suggests resisting vested interests and forging a future outside the lines? Is it a passion for justice that motivates you beyond the prejudice, lethargy, and politics of our resistant world? Is it a professional ethic that demands you stand up to the status quo, calls you to risk money and advancement in order to do what is right and to keep your integrity intact? Today Jesus models and mandates for us a sense of *must*. What is it in your life that is worth living for? What is it in your life that is worth dying for? What is it in your life that you simply *must* do?

Our text suggests that Jesus pauses for just a moment in the midst of his mission and his *must*. He pauses and spreads the wings of his imagination with an image of pathos and love. Glancing from the Mount of Olives across the Kidron Valley looking toward Jerusalem he says, "Jerusalem, Jerusalem, the city that kills the prophets and stones those who are sent to it! How often have I desired to gather your children together as a hen gathers her brood under her wings, and you were not willing!" (v. 34). Because I cannot force you to come, because you are unwilling to grab the rope and pull yourselves toward life, and because you are not willing to come and accept the protection, warmth, and promise of God's nurturing love, I must go on. I must leave you dangling and leave you out in the cold and the dark. I *must* go on and you will not see me again until it is too late, until the palm branches have been swept up, until the bread has been broken, until the nails have been hammered, and my broken body has been laid to rest. Maybe after I have gone through my pain and you have gone through yours, maybe then you will come to me and gather under me and with me around the table of God's kingdom — God's healed and reconciled and empowered kingdom.

Today and always, Jesus gives us a choice. He invites us to gather under his wings, to accept the grace and the freedom and the truth of the Christian life. But we, stubborn and self-destructive, often refuse to go. We, instead, jump over to the side of life's seductions and temptations and away from God and toward despair. Then tying ourselves to our neediness, we beg Jesus, we tempt God, we bargain with the holy one to come with us into the pit of our own destruction. When God refuses to wallow with us, we try to tie Jesus down, stopping his *must* with our maybes. But Jesus will not, cannot, stop to reinforce our dependency or our fear. Instead he gives us a choice. We can travel with him toward the uncertainty of the future, protected by the wide expanse of his gathering wings, or we can stay behind and destroy ourselves.

Scripture tells us that as Jesus continued on his way to Jerusalem, he kept his wings outstretched. He kept his breast bare and vulnerable. We know that he stretched out on a cross — continuing to invite us to be part of his brood — even as the spear pierced his side and he was wounded by a love-starved world. The promise of this season of Lent is that the holy *must* turns into the holy mystery, and through the grace and power of God, Jesus draws us away from our pain toward his so that in and through his struggle we might be healed. It only happens if we choose to go with him. If we choose to pull ourselves up from our destructive dependency and our dangling despair and gather under his wing as we march off to the promise and the pain of Jerusalem.

A rural firefighter tells the story of battling a fierce blaze that was consuming a country barn. Later, the weary worker discovered a poignant scene, beneath the charred remains of a hen, he found intact a bedraggled nest filled with chattering chicks.

"Jerusalem, Jerusalem… How often have I desired to gather your children together as a hen gathers her brood under her wings, but you were not willing?" (v. 34). My friends, are we willing? Are we willing to choose, to decide, to go to Jerusalem under the wings of God's promise? Or will we stay dangling over the precipice of our own discontent? Jesus will go with us or without us. The choice is ours.

May it be so, for you and for me. Amen.

Lent 3
Luke 13:1-9

Stuff Happens

It was probably the most irresponsible decision I have ever made. We'll call her Sarah. She was a college sophomore — energetic, intelligent, passionate about justice, faith, and God. I was serving as Chaplain of Wellesley College, and Sarah was one of my student interns. We lived in the same dorm — me in a faculty apartment, and Sarah in a student room on the third floor. That January term, the college had shut down most of the buildings to save on energy costs, and so we were living in another dorm for a few weeks. One day Sarah mentioned that she needed some clothing in her regular dorm room. Since I had a key, she asked if I would walk over with her and let her into the locked building. I agreed. When we got to the dorm we both went in, I to my apartment and Sarah to her room. After checking on things I left the building not giving a thought to whether Sarah had left or not. Half an hour later, campus security showed up in my study. Sarah needed me. She was in the security office, shaking and in tears. It seems that when she got to her third floor room, she was accosted by a strange man who had been lurking in the abandoned building. With a stocking over his face, he proceeded to rape Sarah and then he quickly left her behind. In just fifteen minutes, Sarah's life disintegrated, and I, naively and unwittingly, had set her up for it.

After this episode, Sarah went through some predictable stages. First, she blamed herself. After some excellent work with a rape crisis counselor, she was able to move beyond that destructive place. She then turned toward me and blamed me for my poor judgment in letting her into the building and then leaving her there alone. We talked about it, I agreed with her assessment, and I apologized again and again. But for years this blaming went on until Sarah realized that blaming me didn't lead to healing or even to the heart of the question "Why?" Twenty-five years later, Sarah is still having a hard time getting her life together. She has moved in and out of churches. She has moved in and out of relationships. She has moved in and out of jobs. But the questions still remain. Where were you, God? Why, God? Why me? Why do bad things happen to a good person like me?

These are the same questions Jesus is asked even today. Why, Jesus? Why were those particular Galileans murdered by Pilate in an act of terrorism? Were they bad people? Were their sins greater than other people's sins? Why, Jesus? Why were those eighteen innocent people killed when the tower at Siloam toppled onto an unsuspecting crowd? Had those folks done something particularly awful that led God to punish them?

Each one of us could probably add our own examples. Why, God? Why does my father, my brother, my husband have terminal, terrible, tyrannical cancer? Why, God? Why did my grandchild die before she was even six months old? Was it my fault? Was I being punished? Why, God? Why was my job eliminated? Why did I end up in such a dysfunctional family? Why did my child get stuck in such an unsavory crowd? Why, God? Why, on a Friday morning, did a tornado rip through that particular trailer park in Georgia? Were those people picked out through some sort of divine lottery to endure tragedy, injury, and death? Jesus, come on. Tell me, tell us, why?

When Jesus answers these questions we hear good news and bad news. The good news is simple: you don't suffer, the people you love don't suffer because of your sin. God doesn't cause bad things to happen to good people. God is not the great disciplinarian in the sky punishing us for our mistakes, judging us for our ignorance, blaming us for our imperfections, and reminding us of our misjudgments. But having delivered this good news, Jesus counter punches with what sounds like bad news or at least very troubling news. God doesn't punish us or make us suffer arbitrarily. *But*, Jesus says, if you do not repent, you, too will perish like the unfortunate victims of Pilate and like the unlucky corpses buried under the ruins of Siloam. What did Jesus mean by these words?

In his best-selling book of a few years ago, Rabbi Harold Kushner, tries to figure out why bad things happen to good people. Specifically he tries to figure out why he and his wife, fierce and faithful Jews, lost their thirteen-year-old son to progeria, a devastating disease that ages a body over night and leads to painful and premature death. Kushner's answer to this basic question about suffering is interesting. He decides that God cannot be all-powerful **and** all-loving. His thinking goes something like this: If God is all-powerful, then that means God causes all the suffering and agony in the world. Such a God, for Kushner, is unthinkable. So, the answer must be that God is *not* all-powerful. This all-loving, always compassionate God is unable to prevent suffering and pain. Instead, God chooses always to be with us in the midst of the agony — sharing the pain of what a powerless God has been unable to prevent. Kushner's answer is intriguing, but from a Christian perspective, he does not go quite deep enough.

If you think about it, Jesus was the personification of Kushner's question. Why did the worst thing of all happen to this very best person? Yet, in his words this morning and in his example on the cross Jesus refuses to honor or answer the question why. You see, for him, the why is not important. In the mind and experience of Jesus, stuff just happens. In a world shaped by God's creativity, freedom is central to the energy of that creativity and freedom means that God gives up some control and power — not because God is impotent, but because God is loving. In other words, an all-powerful God allows evil and suffering in order to preserve the freedom of creation. Stuff happens in the creative energy, the randomness, and the freedom of natural law. Stuff happens in the perverse human freedom of moral law. And being true to the promise of freedom, God does not intervene. That doesn't mean God doesn't care. Or that God is absent. Far from it. In fact, fear, intrigue, jealousy, and ambition ends up nailing God to a cross. What does God do? God embraces the suffering. God endures the suffering. God confronts the suffering. And God transforms the suffering into the creativity of new life. The question is not "why? Why do bad things happen to good people?" The question is "how?" How do we live and how do we endure in a world where stuff simply happens?

This is why Jesus says "Repent or you will perish like they did." Repent means to turn. Turn away from the "why" question and turn toward the "how" question. Turn away from blaming those in authority, blaming God, or blaming the victims. Instead turn and stay close to God. Stay grounded and connected to God's grace. Then when stuff happens — and certainly it will — God can and will sustain you. God will hang from the crosses of your tragedy and your deception, your doubt and your despair. God will weep with you, and God will never abandon you. You will suffer. You will die. But you will not perish unloved and alone when you turn and stay close to God.

Jesus finishes this morning by telling the parable of the fig tree. He tells this story in order to remind us just what kind of God we have. God is not like a landowner who rips us up and throws us out when we don't produce good fruit. No. Instead, God is like a wise and patient gardener who gives us a second and a third and a fourth chance to root ourselves in holy ways. God prunes, digs, and fertilizes us and then waits for the seeds of divine creativity in us to finally blossom into a fruitful life for the world. Yes, far from a God who topples towers and murders innocent Galileans, our God is a gardener who has all the time in the world for us to grow into spiritual maturity and ripeness. Who knows? In God's wisdom, the "stuff" that happens — the seemingly unfair pain, suffering, and distress in the world — this "stuff" may just be the manure that gives nourishment to our developing souls.

Martin Gray was a survivor of the Warsaw Ghetto and the Holocaust. Following the war, he married, raised a family, and became successful in business. Once again, tragedy struck in his life. One day his wife and children were all killed in a forest fire that swept through their home in south France. He was devastated after this senseless loss, and friends encouraged him to launch an investigation into how and why this horror had happened. Instead, Martin Gray began a passionate effort to protect nature from senseless fires. He explained to his friends that an investigation would focus only on the past, on issues of loss and anger and blame, and on accusing other people of being responsible for his misery. He wasn't interested in asking "Why?" He was only interested in asking "Now what?" How can I live into the future — in life-affirming and not life-denying ways? How can I "live for something and not just against something?" (as told by Harold Kushner, *When Bad Things Happen to Good People* [Avon, 1981], p. 136).

Jesus presents us with the central dilemma, the choice, of Lent. Are we stuck in the past or do we believe in the future? Are we living against something or are we living for something? Do we want answers or do we want God? Langston Hughes, writing "Feet o' Jesus" out of the pathos of the African-American experience, dissolves the complexity of this choice with simple words of faith.

At the feet o' Jesus, Sorrow like a sea.
Lordy, let yo' mercy Come driftin' down on me.
At the feet o' Jesus At yo' feet I stand.
O, ma little Jesus, Please reach out yo' hand.

This day, Jesus is reaching out his hand and offering to lift us from our sea of sorrow and from our confusion and our pain. Offering to lift us and turn us toward the mercy and grace of God. This is the good news of the gospel.

May it be so, for you and for me this day and in the days and weeks to come. Amen.

Lent 4
Luke 15:1-3, 11b-32

Holy Hospitality

They are my favorite words in scripture. A holy mantra that I repeat to myself — particularly at those moments when I am stuck in spiritual darkness — those moments when I am yearning for the light. "If anyone is in Christ, there is a new creation: Everything old has passed away; see, everything has become new!" Years ago, for a short while, I lost my faith. I pushed God away because my God had become a God of judgment and duty. I rejected for a while a faith that was based on shoulds and oughts — a faith that could no longer feed my soul. During a worship service these words from Paul literally saved my life. In what was a moment of utter despair, I heard these words spoken quietly, warmly, emphatically deep in my heart: "If you are in Christ, you will be a new creation; the old God is past and gone, and a new God has come." And then the voice continued: "God is not a harsh, judgmental, rejecting God. No, God is available, open, inviting, gracious. And if you can crawl inside the story of Jesus, if you can touch him and listen to him and trust him and know him, then you will be reborn and you will discover your value and the purpose of your life." To this day, those same words still echo whenever I am tired, whenever I am sad, whenever I am ready to throw in the towel of faith, hope, or love. Of course, like most of you, I am still waiting for the new creation to be complete in me and in God's world. In my cynical moments I still wonder if it even exists. Then I read today's gospel lesson, and I know that new creation in God is possible.

One interpreter (John Dominic Crossan) has suggested that the story of the prodigal son is the "essential Jesus," the "bedrock" of the gospel message. To me, this story is, quite simply, the embodiment of God. I have become convinced that the story is misnamed. It is not just the story of one lost son. It is the story of two lost sons. One son lost in out-of-control appetite, and the other son lost in out-of-control resentment. Yet the main character in this story is not either of the brothers. The main character is the father — the prodigal father if you will. This father breaks all the rules of fairness, protocol, inheritance of accountability, and lineage. He refuses to get bogged down in patriarchal shoulds and oughts. He refuses to get mired in self-righteous blaming or tit-for-tat parenting. This father offers love, not a lecture. He throws a party, not a tantrum. He communicates joy, not judgment. This father is created in the imagination of Jesus and acted out in the sacrifice of Jesus. This father makes clear to us that on the scale of God's justice there is no "balance." Grace always outweighs judgment. God's love is unconditional, unequivocal, and inexhaustible. Nothing in life or in death can separate us from God's welcoming arms.

The older brother, the responsible, dutiful, "follow all the rules" brother is, of course, a voice in our own hearts. He doesn't believe this story, doesn't want this story. In fact, he is infuriated by the lavish, extravagant, and spontaneous love of the father. We — those of us who relish the resentment of the older brother — cry out in fury. "It is not fair!" We have followed all the shoulds and oughts. We have played by all the rules. We have done what daddy and mommy want us to do. We have paid our mortgages, been faithful to our spouses, saved our money, sacrificed and served others. We have been over-worked and under-loved. We are the ones who deserve to be God's favorite, to be the father's favorite, to be the church's favorite, to be the company's favorite.

Hey, God, this love you give to that foolish, flagrant failure, "It's just not fair."

The truth of the matter is that God has no favorites. The "good little boy" and the "good little girl" don't get any more love, any more grace, any more reward than the "bad" boys and the "bad" girls. However — and this is important to hear — they don't get any less either. You see, we don't have an either/or God. We have a both/and God — a God who loves sinners and saints, which is a good thing. Because no matter how hard we try in be perfect, no matter how hard we try to be in control, no matter how hard we try to be "good," we fall short of the glory of God. We all squander the inheritance, we all fall into loose living, we all wander away from our home in God. Thanks be to the holy one who loves us and welcomes us whether we are lost in irresponsibility, lost in duty, lost in aimlessness, or lost in resentment. All we need do is admit that we are lost and come home.

Can we stand this kind of God? Can we stand a God who loves loose people as well as livid people? Can we stand a God who welcomes losers as well as winners? A God who welcomes difficult people, annoying people, unpleasant people? Can we stand a God who loves the difficult, the annoying, the unpleasant parts of us? And can we own that image of God in us that calls us to love others with this same lavish, unmerited grace?

Henri Nouwen sees this rich and unsettling story in Luke as the most vivid portrait of God in scripture. Why? Because it illumines the central quality of God's activity in the world. What is that central quality? Hospitality. Nouwen understands that the main work of the Christian faith is transforming *hostis* into *hospis* — transforming hostility and brokenness into hospitality and welcome. The main work of the church is to provide sacred space — physical space, emotional space, spiritual space, intellectual space — so that people can find a new home, a comfortable home in God.

Rodger Nishioka, a professor at Columbia Theological Seminary, has been working with young adults in the PCUSA for over 25 years. He wrote his doctoral dissertation on the disappearing Gen Xers and Millennials in our pews. He put together a list of over 2,000 young adults in their twenties and thirties who were confirmed in our congregations but are no longer with us, and he interviewed 200 of them. His question to them was simple: What needs to happen in our Presbyterian congregations for you to come back to church?

The most significant experience our drop-out children are yearning for is hospitality — a welcome so engaging and real and intentional that there is no question that they — and every other person, weird or not — is part of the church's family. We are not talking here about a quick handshake at the door or a smile from across the room. We are talking about a welcome that invites the story — hungers, failures, needs, ideas, gifts, questions, music, clothes, and lifestyles of each person as crucial and essential in order for the church to be complete.

In these post-modern days, the call to evangelism — so clear in scripture — is rooted in this kind of extravagant hospitality. Who is missing in our pews and why? How do we change and melt and open up and reach out in order to radically welcome every child of God?

Each community of faith needs to ask some hard questions. How welcoming are we to each other? To our children? To strangers who walk through our door? Are we, in any sense, an "older brother" kind of church: judgmental, suspicious, resentful of those who saunter in here with shallow commitment and loose living? Do we judge those who don't understand our theology, who may not always appreciate our music, who may not understand our traditions? Do we panic when an immigrant, who speaks little English, begins to worship in our midst?

There is a second level of questions. Within the community that is already here, how hospitable are we to the strangers already in our midst? Do we know the names of those who always sit two pews over and one pew back? Who is that young mother who sits in front of us with her two, three, or four children? Are we annoyed because the little ones squirm and whisper during the sermon or are we curious enough about this woman and her needs that we reach out to her, talking with her and maybe offering to sit with her and to encourage her children? If we are a musical person, do we know and respect the mission people in our midst? If we're a mission person, do we acknowledge the "mission" of the singer? The "mission" of the Sunday school teacher? Or do we feel that the only "mission" that matters is feeding and touching the poor?

As we sink into this familiar story of grace in scripture, who are we in the story? Are we lost in loose living? Are we lost in rigidity and resentment? Are we incarnating the radical hospitality and the radical grace of our radical God?

Thirty years ago, when my husband and I were first starting to co-pastor in our new congregation in New Jersey, I felt like a total stranger, a young mother with a six-month-old baby trying to figure out how to juggle marriage, ministry, and mothering. Our call to become co-pastors at that congregation had been controversial at best with 15% of the vote going against us. Much of the suspicion and hostility was centered on me. After all, a pushy woman in ministry was an alien concept for those blue collar workers in Italian New Jersey. The first several weeks, I put on a brave public face but then I would go home and cry, fret, and wallow in my anxiety and my frustration.

One day, the doorbell rang. I opened the door and there stood Pearl — the ring leader of the group that had voted against us. Pearl was carrying three things: a loaf of bread, a pinch of salt, and a broom. Nervously, she smiled and offered her odd gifts to me: the bread to welcome me, the pinch of salt for good luck, and the broom to sweep away all the evil spirits. My friends, that morning Pearl killed the fatted calf for me. She welcomed the lost part of me into the home of her heart. Yes, an old German house warming custom broke the ice between us and transformed hostility into hospitality. Pearl and I never agreed on much during my ten years in that congregation. But we stayed connected because of the holy hospitality she offered to me when I was lost and needed to be found.

My friends, this day and every day God stands with open arms waiting to welcome us home, reaching out to us in the midst of our lostness and our brokenness. Each day, God through Christ offers us a new creation of wholeness, healing, and welcome. Each day God calls us to be agents of reconciliation and hosts of grace for each other and for the world. This is the good news of the gospel.

May it be so for you and for me. Amen.

Lent 5
John 12:1-8

Time Out

In that wonderful movie *Steel Magnolias*, Shelley, the hair dresser, offers us some good advice. "I'd rather have a half hour of wonderful," she says, "than a whole life time of nothing special." This is a sentiment that might well be echoed by Mary as she unbinds her long, sensuous hair in this morning's gospel lesson. On the liturgical calendar, this fifth Sunday of Lent is traditionally called "Laudate Sunday" — the day in more liturgical traditions when the purple hangings are replaced by pink hangings or "bubblegum Sunday," as some have irreverently called it. In the dark, dense journey of Lent, from wilderness ash to Calvary cruelty, today is "time out" Sunday — an invitation to take time out for affection, adoration, fragrant joy, and love. As such, this Sunday gives us a model, a rhythm of faithfulness that can help us endure all the dark and treacherous valleys of our living.

A columnist for the *Los Angeles Times*, Ann Lewis, recalls a conversation she had with her brother-in-law in the days between her sister's death and the funeral. They were standing in the bedroom. Her brother-in-law reached into the bottom draw of his wife's bureau and pulled out a tissue wrapped package. He opened it and handed it to Ann — an exquisite slip — pure silk trimmed with handmade lace. The price tag was still on the slip — an extravagant amount of money. It seems that Ann's sister was saving the slip for a special occasion and never even put it on. The brother-in-law took the slip back and put it with the rest of the clothes they were taking to the funeral home. With bitter sadness, he slammed the drawer shut, and proclaimed the message of today's gospel story. *"Don't ever save anything for a special occasion. Every day you're alive is a special occasion"* (date unknown).

Mary instinctively understands this when this morning she anoints, she touches, and honors Jesus with a jar of exquisite perfume — spikenard worth over one year's wages. The death of her brother Lazarus has taught Mary the unpredictability of life, and the miracle of his resurrection just a few days later has astonished her with the graciousness of God. So overwhelmed by gratitude, transformed by mystery, filled with affection for the one who gives the daily gift of life, Mary takes time out — time out to worship, to say thank you, to acknowledge the holy, and to offer herself — body and soul — to the God she sees in Jesus.

Wasteful. That is Judas' response and probably ours, too, if we are honest. Think about it in our context. Two thousand dollars for an orchestra on Music Sunday? Sixty thousand dollars for two new stained-glass windows? Building renovations and improvement at $1.75 million? So much money spent on ourselves, our building, and our worship when hundreds of children die of violence and neglect every year ten miles from our front door. Is this not, in Judas' words, "wasteful"? Is the affection and awe expressed through music, the glow of grace that bathes us through stained glass, the comfort and strength we receive within the walls of a building appropriate when the poor, who we always have with us, are suffering?

I'm not sure that Mary thought all of this through when she knelt and anointed the feet of Jesus, instinctively offering to him her love, her touch, her adoration, and her gratitude. This was not premeditated waste. It was spontaneous worship honoring the worth of God with the very richest part of herself — her heart. I wonder, do we ever say "I love you" to God with the passion, intensity, and completeness with which Mary says it this morning? Are we that aware, grateful, and overwhelmed by the sheer gift of life?

Several years ago, *Time* magazine interviewed Bill Gates, who we all know is one of the richest man in America. Having grown up a Congregationalist, Gates is currently a church drop out along with two thirds of his generation. His reason? It is a waste of time. "Just in terms of allocation of time resources, religion is not very efficient. There's a lot more I could be doing on Sunday morning," he told the magazine (1/13/97). That, of course, is true for all of us. Eleven o'clock Sunday morning. The laundry needs to be done. The garden is a mess. This is the only time I have to jog. The malls are open, the sports teams are calling, and the Post sits there just begging to be read. Worship? What a waste of time particularly when the hymns are boring, the preacher is having an off Sunday, and I don't seem to get anything out of it.

However, Mary, when she worships this morning, doesn't expect "to get anything out of it." She worships because she has to, because she wants to and not because she expects to "receive" something. She needs to give something of herself — her heart, her time, her love, her gratitude, her affection. Yes, she needs to take time out to say "thank you" to God.

We humans tend to divide ourselves into two groups: the scarcity folks and the abundance folks. The scarcity folks believe that everything is limited: love, grace, generosity, time, money. If we let go of anything, share anything, spontaneously give away anything, there won't be enough left for us. The abundance folks see life differently. Whether it's love, hope, grace, money, time, worldly goods — when it's gone it's gone, what we have is enough, and when we need more, it will come. For the abundance folks, life is inherently grace filled. Mary is part of the second group. It's not that she's wasteful. It's just that she's grace filled. When the nard is gone, it's gone. What she has without it is enough. When she needs more — for her own needs or someone else's — she trusts that she will receive more.

When Judas excoriates Mary this morning, Jesus responds by quoting from Deuteronomy 15, but he only quotes half the verse. Yes, Moses says to the people of Israel: "You will always have the poor with you." But the rest of the verse is equally important: "Therefore I command you, 'Open your hand to the poor and needy neighbor in your land' " (v. 11). What Jesus suggests this morning is that when we learn to be gracious and extravagant in our love, our worship, our gratitude, and our adoration of God, then we are learning to be abundant folk in all areas of our living. We are learning to be people who can also be gracious, generous, and extravagant in our care and concern for others — learning to be people who can be as lavish in our mission outreach as we are in our worship and care for ourselves.

A German Jew named Gerda Klein remembers her friend Ilse whom she met in a concentration camp during World War II. It seems that one day Ilse found a raspberry — one fresh raspberry — an unheard of luxury in the sterile, fruitless atmosphere of the camps. Rather than eating it, Ilse carried this treasure in her pocket all day. In the evening, she offered it to Gerda — one tender berry resting like a jewel on a small green leaf. "Imagine a world in which your entire possession is one raspberry," writes Gerda, "and you give it to a friend" (source unknown). This is love, extravagant love, like exotic perfume poured out lavishly in order to honor the gift of life.

Mary, of course, pre-shadows the events of the next two weeks when we move beyond Laudate Sunday back into the death valley of Lent. When, in the week we call "holy," the most extravagant, wasteful gift of all is given. This Lord whom Mary anoints with perfume will soon anoint us with his blood — pouring out his life that we might have new abundant life. Unafraid to live where we live, to suffer where we suffer, to weep where we weep, to die where we die, this Jesus walks with us every step of the way — forgiving us, changing us, empowering us, and recreating us with an abundance of life and grace that can never be depleted. The only price we pay for the extravagance of Jesus is our heart offered on bended knee. The offering of ourselves as a daily living sacrifice — faithful and fragrant as his disciples.

This morning recommit yourselves to be generous, spontaneous, and extravagant — to be wasteful — in your discipleship for God.

May it be so, for you and for me. Amen.

Passion / Palm Sunday
Luke 22:14—23:56

The Tears of God

Let me tell you a story about two oak trees. One stood right on the edge of the prairie. The other, surrounded by water, grew from a log in the springhole. Each year when the fires came sweeping across the plains, the Prairie Edge Oak lost its leaves and was badly scarred on its ugly and increasingly twisted trunk. But the Springhole Oak, surrounded and protected by water, remained pure, beautiful, and lovely. "You're a disgrace to the rest of us," the Springhole Oak said to the deformed Prairie Edge Oak.

Then came the winter of the rabbits, and with their voracious gnawing, the hungry little beasts lit into the trunks of the two trees. The scarred, thick layers of the Prairie Edge Oak were impossible to break through and so the homely tree was spared destruction. When the rabbits hopped over to the Springhole Oak, the little tree that had seen neither trial nor tribulation was sweet and soft to the touch — and was soon ripped apart by sharp little teeth. The Prairie Edge Oak survived one more year and grew ever stronger despite its scars. The Springhole Oak slowly withered of its wounds and finally, since it had never known adversity, it died (as told by Elaine Ward, *The Art of Storytelling* [Brea, California: Educational Ministries, Inc., 1990], p. 60).

Today, we begin the strangest week of the Christian year. A week that the world does not understand. A week that we don't understand. Jesus dies for our sins? Through the suffering and blood of the cross we inherit eternal life? What does all of this mean? After all these years, I still haven't figured it all out — particularly the sin and the blood part. But the suffering part? That makes a whole lot of sense. Scarred and tenacious, with love in his eyes, Jesus enters, endures, and survives adversity. He proves without a shadow of a doubt that nothing in all of life or death can separate us from the love of God.

I don't know about you, but I'm tired of Lent. Not tired in the sense of being bored but tired in the sense of being exhausted. I made the decision that this year we would explore Luke's passion story in depth, and so we have spent six weeks slogging through the details of Luke's final chapters. It has been rough going. We cringed as the disciples bickered about who was more important and who was more loved. We nodded off with those same disciples as they fell asleep in the garden at that very moment when Jesus needed their companionship the most. We lurked in the shadows, impotent and scared, as Judas did his dastardly deed. We wept bitterly with Peter after his desperate denial, not once, not twice, but three times. Earlier today we were swept up in the crowd, stamping, waving, and screaming at superstar Jesus. Only to change our tune when the crowd gets ugly railing at this Lord who drags us into darkness in order to uncover the light. I think, after six weeks, the message is clear. Somewhere in this story each one of us has built a home. Whether we like it or not, we have come face-to-face with the shadow side of our own living.

This morning we meet two last pathetic figures in this sorry cast of Passion characters. With presidential campaigns still sour to the taste, partisan political stench still permeating the air, it is not hard to believe the saga of Pilate and Herod. It's not that they are bad people. They are just very human. It is interesting to note that in the Apostle's Creed, the only four words that describe Jesus' earthly life relate to today's gospel lesson: "He suffered under Pontius Pilate..." Yes, it seems that it is in the depth of our muddy humanness that the very human Jesus suffers.

Actually, Luke's portrayal of Pilate is much more positive than any of the other gospels. Three times he tries to get Jesus off the hook and three times the crowd eggs him on. He knows that Jesus is innocent. But, as is often the case, innocence does not matter. When fear, jealousy, and power are on the line, what is fair, just, and right often gets lost. For one tantalizing moment, Pilate foists Jesus off on Herod hoping he can avoid the messy decision that is ahead of him. But Herod gets mired in the same mess with an innocent man and an angry crowd. What follows is one of the strangest and most chilling sentences in all of scripture: "That same day Herod and Pilate became friends with each other; before this they had been enemies" (v. 23:12). How easy it is to become friends with expedience, compromise, and ambition — all at the expense of that which is good and right.

What finally emerged for me this week after forty days of pain and passion is Luke's stunning portrait of Jesus. In Matthew, a strident Jesus keeps quoting the law and prophets. In Mark, a foreboding Jesus keeps making dire predictions about his death. In John, a dazzling glorified Jesus rises above the fray with eloquent theological piety and poetry. But in Luke, a serene Jesus remains essentially quiet: mute and magnificent. Jesus stands there, elegantly rooted in the midst of it all. He doesn't chastise the disciples. He doesn't argue with Pilate. He doesn't agonize on the cross. In Luke, Jesus does not argue, defend, blame, negotiate, retaliate, or explain. Instead, he stands firmly, he gazes unflinchingly, he loves unconditionally, and he dies peacefully. It is in Luke that the final words caress us instead of scream at us. Those words of Jesus from the cross are the familiar cadences of a Hebrew child's bedside player: "Father, into thy hands I commend my Spirit" (Luke 23:46).

In Luke's gospel, Jesus is neither in agony nor in conflict. Instead, strong and serene, he knows who he is and he refuses to be *less* than he is. This rock-solid honesty and integrity puts a stark mirror in front of each one of us. Jesus shows us the worst of who we are and the best of who we can be.

The film *Remember the Titans* can serve as a perfect entree into the drama of Holy Week. It not a great movie but it is a good story — a morality tale that judges us, much like Jesus' steady gaze in Luke's gospel. It is, of course, the retelling of the integration at T.C. Williams High School in Alexandria, Virginia, in the early sixties, focusing on the trial and tribulations of the school's football team. Denzel Washington portrays Coach Boone, the token black brought in to fulfill a court order, but he is also a scapegoat slated to fail by the racist powers that be.

The most riveting scene in the movie actually involves the white assistant coach, a man who was demoted so that the school board could promote Coach Boone. There is much hatred and tension between these two coaches at the beginning of the movie — just as there is between the white and the black football players. As the plot unfolds and their common commitment to the team binds them together, these two coaches become unlikely and somewhat frosty friends.

In the regional championship, there is intense pressure for the team to lose because a win would somehow give credence to the whole movement toward integration. The referees have been bribed to make sure T.C. Williams loses and all the white coach needs to do is keep his mouth shut. After all, these same athletic officials are just about to name him to the coaches' Hall of Fame — an honor he has been working toward his entire career.

In a breathtaking moment, the white coach's daughter looks at him from the sidelines, aware of what is going on, and she is horrified that her father is about to condone such racist cheating. In that gaze the coach is called back to his better self — befriending that which is good in himself and in the world. He confronts and transforms the cheating. The

Titans win the championship and he loses his Hall of Fame chances forever. The gospel message in a nutshell. The one who loses his life will find it. The battle against evil and prejudice, racism and fear wins one more small skirmish.

As Pilate prevaricates, as Herod humiliates, as the crowd erupts with bloodthirsty cries, Jesus remains calm, serene, and focused. It's not that he really wants to die. It's that he wants the good in him, the good in us, and the good in the world to live. So with a steady gaze, he looks at each one of us and asks us to decide. Who and what will we befriend with the integrity of our lives? Will we embrace compassion, love, justice, and hope? Or will we hide in the security and smallness of our unfinished lives? Will we allow others to define us and the world to diminish us? Will we go along with the crowd? Or will we stand up for the good, the right, and the true — no matter how much it costs us?

Of course, whichever way we decide, Jesus still gazes at us with love. Jesus still stretches out his arms on a long wooden beam — wide enough to hold all of us — turning the cross into a cradle of grace and new life. As Frederick Buechner reminds us, there is nothing *we* have to do. There is nothing we *have* to do. There is nothing we have to *do* in order to earn God's favor. All that is necessary is to return Jesus's gaze with longing and need in our eyes. Whether we are Peter or Judas, Pilate or Herod, whether we are jeering with the crowd or weeping with the women, Jesus weeps, grieves, and suffers with us, accepting us as we really are and loving us into who we can be. The cross is a mystery but most of all it is a gift.

A writer tells of a lady in Charleston who met the negro servant of a neighbor.

> *"I'm sorry to hear of your Aunt Lucy's death," she said. "You must miss her greatly. You were such friends."*
> *"Yes'm," said the servant. "I is sorry she died. But we wasn't no friends."*

"Why?" said the lady. "I thought you were. I've seen you laughing and talking together lots of times."
"Yes'm, that's so," came the reply. "We've laughed together and we've talked together, but we is just quaintances. You see, Miss Ruth, we ain't never shed no tears. Folks got to cry together before dey is friends."

(source unknown)

Brothers and sisters, the only friend we really meet in today's story is Jesus. C.S. Lewis calls Jesus "the tears of God," shed with us and for us, in order to water the soil of abundant life. This week, as we stand at the foot of the cross, let us sense the integrity and the serenity in Jesus' gaze and let us receive the friendship of his tears.

May it be so for you and for me. Amen.

Maundy Thursday
John 13:1-7, 31b-35

Basin Believers

Parker Palmer is a contemporary writer and teacher who plumbs the depth of the human spirit and sinks deeply into the darkness of the Holy Spirit. It is there, in the darkness, that he most often finds the light.

Parker often writes about his own shadow experiences — particularly those years when he lived in the black pit of depression. As he withdrew and wallowed in the darkness, his friends tried to reach out and support him. But most of them just wanted to "fix" him. They tried to cheer him up with food, stories, and laughter. That did not work. They tried to affirm him — lavishing praise for his wonderful accomplishments. That did not work. They tried to confront him, hoping to startle him out of his angst. That did not work. They tried to give him advice, hoping that the wisdom of others might heal him. That did not work. All of these friends were well-intentioned but all of them were avoiding, even denying, Parker's suffering. They simply were not able to be "with him" in his suffering.

Finally one friend came to see him and said nothing. Instead, he sat at Parker's feet, took off Parker's shoes and rubbed his feet. This friend returned often in the next few weeks — just to touch Parker — and to be "with him" in his suffering.

This evening, those of us gathered around the Lord's table have a choice. We can avoid the suffering of the next three days or we can enter, experience, and be healed by it. We can deny and turn away from the pain and the passion, or we can bend and touch it. Which kind of friend will we be?

John's version of the Last Supper is very different than the traditional Maundy Thursday story. In John there is no sacrament of bread and wine. Instead there is the sacrament of the basin — the sacrament of touching feet instead of touching food.

When I first entered parish ministry, I had a half hour ride to the church I served. I always passed a modern Lutheran church, no spire, no stained glass, no grandeur. Instead of a cross, the symbol displayed on the outside wall, for the entire world to see, was a basin and a towel — a message of compassion, calling, and service just as powerful as the message of the cross.

There are some pivotal actors in this drama of Holy Week. All of them turn away from the suffering or deepen the suffering of Jesus except for the women at the tomb, and Jesus himself. Let's consider, for just a moment, Pontius Pilate.

He is one of the most intriguing characters in the script of this week because he is not all bad. He engages Jesus in deep theological conversation, and he begins to sense that this man is not a rabble rouser but someone who knows the truth. When the crowd keeps calling for Jesus' death, Pilate tries — three times — to change their minds. In the end, Pilate has no courage. When he senses that the crowd is bloodthirsty for crucifixion, he caves in. Yes, he takes a basin, fills it with water, and washes his hands of the whole affair. Then he turns Jesus over to the crowd. In the process, Pilate stifles his own compassion. He denies the truth he has just discovered and he avoids suffering — his own suffering. Yet, in the process, he causes the suffering of Jesus to begin.

Jesus, of course, makes a very different decision. He, too, uses a basin, but for a different purpose. Faced with an agonizing death, he does not run away. He does not blame others. He does not negotiate for his life. Instead, in his last supper with his friends, he focuses on them. In one of the loveliest lines in scripture, John reminds us that "Jesus loved them to the end" (v. 1).

Stripping off his robe and reaching for a towel and a basin, Jesus bends down and does the work of a servant. He slowly and tenderly washes the feet of his disciples — shocking them and touching them at the very core of their being.

Jesus becomes naked in order to show us the naked truth. He becomes naked and vulnerable in order to touch the naked and vulnerable parts of who we are. He touches, soothes, and washes the feet of his disciples — past and present — in order to prepare us for the journey. The painful journey to the cross and the painful journey beyond the cross when we will become the ones to bend, touch, and serve.

Suffering is not the point of Christ's passion. Unconditional and emphatic love is the point of Christ's passion. But an inevitable by-product of confronting the powers and principalities of this world is suffering. Of all the world religions, Christianity is the only one that has as its main symbol an instrument of torture and death. Rather than a star, moon, or a sign of peace, Christians are marked by a cross at the moment of our baptism, in the shadows of Ash Wednesday, and often, as a blessing when we are close to death.

As part of my personal spiritual discipline, I wear a cross every day during Lent as a daily reminder of my calling to pick up my cross and follow Jesus. But the cross is also, for me, a symbol of comfort. It is a reminder that there is no suffering you or I or the world endures that Jesus does not endure with us. Yes, those outstretched arms of the cross are not just a symbol of suffering. They also offer an eternal promise. Nothing in life or in death can separate us from the love of God in Christ Jesus our Lord.

The promises of the cross don't stop with our personal salvation. That is why I wish I could find a small basin to add to the cross around my neck. After Jesus washes his disciples' feet, he stands up and offers them an object lesson.

"I give you a new commandment," he says. "Just as I have loved you, you also should love one another" (v. 34). Just as I have bent low to serve you in the most ordinary of circumstances, so you are to bend low to serve the very real needs of very real people wherever we find them.

A cowardly Pilate, his hands still wet from the basin, turns Jesus over to the crowd and the beginning of loneliness, suffering, and death. In contrast, a tender Jesus, his hands still wet from the basin, makes a very different choice. He hands us over to each other and calls us to love each other as extravagantly and unconditionally as God loves us.

As I write these words, I am finishing up a 48-hour private retreat at a Anglican Benedictine monastery, perched on the banks of the Hudson River. My soul has been nourished by solemn liturgies, the quiet rhythm of sung psalms, and simple, nourishing food. Outside the winter sky is weeping as nature's version of lament. This morning I allowed myself the gift of a massage — a body prayer to soothe my aching back. Like the woman anointing Jesus' feet with her hair, like Jesus washing the feet of the disciples, this holy touch from a humble therapist blessed me at a moment of deep need and vulnerability.

Once again, I am reminded that serving others — touching others where they hurt the most — is the call of Christian discipleship. I am reminded through my own discomfort, that the world is full of suffering and pain that makes my own troubles fade in comparison. Recognizing how much I need to be loved when my own strength is at a low point opens me to hear Jesus in a new way. If he can hang broken on across, I can open my heart to feel the pain of the world, and I can re-commit myself to love the suffering of the world, just as God continues to love me.

Holy Week is not a happy time in the liturgical life of the church. But it is a joyful time — a time to celebrate the deep and abundant joy that Jesus experiences in the darkest hours of his life. He finds his deepest gladness in giving his life that others might live. How can I — how can we — do anything less?

So, friends, as we prepare to offer our feet, freely and vulnerably to the touch of one another, the question is set before us. What kind of basin believers will we be? Those who wash our hands of any responsibility in confronting the evils in the world? Or those who gird up our loins, bending low, to wash away the tears of a hurting world? The choice is clear, and the cross looms.

Fierce and frail God, we come before you this night with feeble faith.
You call us to remember; instead we forget.
You call us to pray; instead we daydream.
You call us to serve; instead we turn away.
Loving, living God, this night
feed us once more;
touch us once more;
forgive us once more.
And give us courage to follow you — all the way to the Cross.
We pray in the tender name of Jesus,
Amen.

Good Friday
John 18:1—19:42

In Love with the Cross

The pastor's voice was quiet and somber. But for two years he couldn't speak at all. It was four in the afternoon, July 1997, and the fathers had just come back from their sun-soaked labor in the fields, and the families were reconnecting and getting ready for supper. With no warning, 350 paramilitary soldiers swarmed into town and at gunpoint ordered all the men, women, and children to gather in the town square. No reason. No exception. Two years earlier, an elder in the pastor's Presbyterian congregation had been shot by the paramilitaries, because he sold medicine from his drug store to a guerrilla who had wandered into town. In those days in Colombia, any suspected sympathy with the guerrillas was an invitation to death, so the town had become very careful. But on that golden July afternoon they had begun to relax, which made the massacre all that worse.

As the men cowered in the courtyard awaiting the worst, the children were quickly corralled by the women and taken to the safety of the Catholic church — the only building with secure walls in the village. The pastor, along with all of the men, was lying, face down, frozen in the plaza. That is until one of the paramilitaries — the one with a heart — whispered into the pastor's ear "Run, man, run!" The trance of terror was broken. The pastor ran, followed by others. And so the number murdered was only twelve instead of the sixty it could have been.

Hidden in the woods, the men watched as flames shot up and their village and their church were burned to the ground. Then they hid for three days not knowing if their families were still alive. Soon thereafter, the 3,000 people who survived buried their dead. Then they left the mountain village, taking with them only what they could carry. They wandered toward the big cities that were already overflowing with four million refugees, displaced by the futile violence that threatens to destroy Columbia — a violence that has been made worse by the billions of US dollars given to Columbia in military aid. Our money is supposed to help fight drugs and terrorism. However, there is more coca being grown in Colombia, and more cocaine being snuffed on our American streets than when the "war on drugs" first began. The only terrorism that is visible in Columbia is the desperation of four million people who have only fear to fill their stomachs.

As the pastor spoke, his voice was quiet and somber. For two years he couldn't speak at all. His name, the pastor who watched the crucifixion happen before his eyes, his name was "Hay-sus" — his name was Jesus. Today, in the wilderness of Colombia, he is quietly pastoring the refugees and refusing to give into the temptation of despair. And in the shadow of all the crosses of death, he lives in the hope and promise of the resurrection.

Resurrection work, it seems, is always done in the shadow of the cross — in the shadows of violence, suffering, and human need. The lilies of Easter morning can only grow out of the ashes of death and despair. This is the human story and as Christians, we are called to embrace the story of the cross — to enter it, feel it, endure it, and be transformed within it.

As a candidate for ordained ministry many years ago, I was expected to write a Statement of Faith. I began my testimony with simple words. *"I find my faith at the foot of the cross."* Forty years later, those words still hold true. As a child I always loved Good Friday and looked forward to the three-hour Protestant service from 12 to 3 in the afternoon

— the Seven Last Words of Christ — each "word" embedded in preaching, prayer, and haunting music. My father always preached on one of the words, and my mother always sang "He Was Despised and Rejected" from the *Messiah*. To this day, I can hear her rich contralto weeping with the sorrow of her Lord.

In today's world, parents often try to "protect" their children from any form of darkness — no disturbing news, no depressing story books, no acknowledgment of world tragedies, and no discussion of death, suffering, or pain. I am grateful that I grew up in a home that was real, where the world headlines formed dinner table conversation, where attendance at relative's funerals was expected, where the suffering of people in the congregation were lifted up in prayer, where human suffering was carefully acknowledged rather than buried in avoidance. And instead of shielding us from the Good Friday service, my sister, brother, and I were expected to sit through all three hours. Yet, rather than being terrified, horrified, or traumatized by the details of the crucifixion story, I found myself comforted, embraced, and loved. Somehow the pain of Jesus was always filtered through the love of Jesus, and I began to trust that because of the cross, I was safe, cherished, and worthy. I felt the pain and darkness of the crucifixion. I also felt rescued by love and courage — the love of Jesus, who does not suffer for me but suffers with me whenever life's agonies come my way.

The text for this evening comes from John's account of the crucifixion — the Passion of Saint John — words sung, read, and painted with glory and gratitude throughout the ages. I prefer the passion accounts in Mark, Matthew, and Luke, for it is in those gospels that we *feel* the crucifixion — the bloody sweat in the garden, the gouging pain of the thorns, the weeping over Jerusalem, the cry of abandonment from Jesus on the cross, the compassionate forgiveness offered out of pain, and the despair and devotion of the women at the foot of the cross.

John's version of the passion story is more emotionally neutral as if a reporter is listing the facts, objectively describing each event as it unfolds. Jesus and Pilate have a calm and rational conversation. The soldiers throw the dice in a pedestrian game of chance. Jesus efficiently arranges for his mother's long-term care. The author ticks off Old Testament scripture to anchor each act in the crucifixion drama. The only real "passion" in John's passion play is the blood thirsty rage of the crowd — the blood thirsty cries of fallen humanity — "Crucify him! Crucify him!"

Most of all, it is the tone of John that differs from the other three gospels. This crucifixion is not about violence but about victory. The focus is not on gore but on glory. And the death is not a bitter ending but a magnificent beginning. John's crucifixion is not about humiliation. John's crucifixion is about glorification. The final words, "It is finished," are the exultant proclamation that God's work of salvation is done.

I prefer the emotional immediacy of Matthew and Luke because their Jesus on the cross is accessible and comforting to my imperfect and troubled heart. But the glory of John is becoming more powerful the older I get, for I am beginning to understand that John's Jesus transforms suffering, rather than wallowing in it. John's Jesus gives the refugees in Colombia and Christians in Palestine and the soldiers in Afghanistan — John's Jesus gives you and me — the power and the hope to persevere. John's Jesus gives us the courage and the compassion to practice resurrection even in the shadow of the cross.

How do we integrate the humility of the cross with the victory of the cross? How do we balance the suffering of the cross with the glory of the cross? How do we reconcile the two, somewhat contradictory, "words" of Jesus from the cross — both the quiet prayer of Luke "Lord, into your hands I commit my Spirit," and the victory cry of John, "It is finished"?

Years ago I traveled to Israel and Palestine with a small group of pilgrims, intent on experiencing the land of Jesus through the perspective and experience of Palestinian Christians. We ended our troubling journey on the island of Cyprus and visited an ancient monastic cave, tucked into a cliff high above the jeweled sea. It was not an easy climb and the entrance into the cave was difficult. Yet, it was in this rugged place that holy men had spent their entire lives spanning several centuries.

Bending down we squeezed into the outer chamber of the cave, only to find a simple mat, table, and chair. However, there was another chamber — an inner chamber — that could only be reached by dropping down and crawling on our knees.

When we reached that inner room all we could do was lie on our backs and look up. And there, splashed across the jagged ceiling, was a magnificent mural of the Pantocrator — Christ as king — serene beauty, a shimmering blue robe, and a gentle smile. It was the eyes, however, that most filled me with awe and wonder, holy eyes, loving eyes that penetrated deep within my soul.

The two finger blessing in that mural — central to any image of the Pantocrator — was a pivotal blessing in my life. The little girl comforted by the sad music and reassuring compassion of Good Friday was joined by a middle-aged woman, beginning to fully understand the redeeming power of crucifixion and the hopeful promise of resurrection. Though my life is not finished, and God's creation is not finished, I realized in that cave that for Jesus, his earthly mission found completion on the cross. His work was finished. His life — and ours — was worth all the bane and blessing of that fateful day.

But what Jesus has "finished," we are still engaged in. Through the power of resurrection, we continue the humble, glorious, and costly work of Jesus — giving our lives daily so that God's dream can live. My prayer is that when it comes time for our last breath, we will be able to say "It is finished!" because our purpose for being on earth will have been fulfilled.

May it be so for you and for me. Amen.

Easter Day
John 20:1-18

Telling the Truth

Alleluia! Christ is risen! Alleluia!

This is the first time in 35 years that I don't feel the need to "explain" the resurrection. In fact I'm not even going to try to give rational credence to the biological absurdity of this day. Instead, I simply want to proclaim resurrection, to proclaim, against all rational odds, that God has done it again.

God, out of nothing, has created everything! God, out of emptiness, has created the abundance of exquisite life!

I have discovered over the years that a preacher's job on Easter is not to focus on facts but on faith. Not to unravel science but to unleash Spirit. Not to dwell on the past but to open up the future. In other words, the burden and privilege of this day is not to offer the proof of resurrection, but instead to proclaim the truth of resurrection. What a joy it is for me to do so!

If you think about it, truth is a rare commodity in today's world. Most of us have an ax to grind or a flaw to cover up when we try to tell the truth. Just think mortgage brokers and massive foreclosures or George W. Bush and weapons of mass destruction. Yes, truth is hard to tell in our win-at-all-cost world.

I went to my biblical concordance on Friday and discovered an interesting fact about the word "truth" in scripture. The word appears once in Matthew, twice in Luke, and three times in Mark. But it appears 22 times in the gospel of John — one of the main themes in this second-century account of

Jesus' life. John's birth narrative is that elegant description of the "word becoming flesh," dwelling among us, full of grace and truth. Then the gospel writer goes on encouraging us to stop focusing on empty ritual and to instead worship "in spirit and in truth." In one of his more direct sermons, Jesus makes it clear that we are to know the truth, for only "the truth will set us free." Then he puts content to his words by reminding us that he, Jesus, is the way, the truth, and the life. The last time we hear the word "truth" in the gospel of John is in the passion story. Pilate asks the wounded, haunted, humiliated Jesus: "What is truth?" And the answer Jesus gives is completely silent, but profound. The answer Jesus gives is to immediately enter into his forgiving death and his liberating resurrection. In John's gospel, the truth is God's glorious, gutsy, ghastly gift of grace embodied in the flesh and blood of Jesus Christ.

So, for me, the resurrection tells the truth — the truth about life — your life, my life, and the life of the world. And the foundational truth of truth is this — God is in charge of life — not you or me, not Barack Obama or Vladimir Putin, not the Dow Jones average or your SAT score, not family or friends, not your boss or your physician or your accountant. No, God is in charge of life and that is good news indeed.

Do some of you remember, back in the 1970s when Alvin Toffler wrote his book *Future Shock*? He had all kinds of predictions about technology, education, community life, politics, and economics. At about the same time a seminary held a conference inviting the avant garde scholars of the day to gather and do "futuring" about the church based on Toffler's predictions. The seminary president was asked to give the closing address at that conference and this is what he said: "I am only a theologian, and I have no idea what shape the future will take. The only thing I do know is that the future will belong to a merciful God." Recently that retired seminary president found his notes from that conference. "You know," he said, "I was the only one whose prediction was right!" (paraphrased from a sermon by Thomas G. Long, "Growing Old and Wise on Easter").

William Sloan Coffin was a giant in the last half of the twentieth century: a civil rights activist, Chaplain of Yale University, Preacher at Riverside Church in New York City, and president of a major Nuclear Freeze organization. In his last few years, Coffin was severely restricted from a stroke and quietly awaiting his death with anticipation and little regret. In a pre-death, reflective interview, Coffin remembered what it was like when he was a not-particularly religious college student. He attended a memorial service for two of his friends who had been killed in an automobile accident and something he heard caught Coffin off balance. The priest intoned familiar words: "The Lord giveth and the Lord taketh away." It was the giveth part that pierced Coffin's soul — his prideful, puffed up, young adult, "I'm in charge of the world" soul. And that simple phrase changed his life: "I just thought, 'You know, Coffin, you're only a guest here... a guest, at best' " (interview with Alexa Smith of the Presbyterian News Service, April 7, 2004).

The truth of resurrection, my friends, is simply that God is in charge, creating us, re-creating us, chastening us, challenging us, chastising us, cherishing us with fresh surprises every morning. Either we can resist and rebel, trying unsuccessfully to wrest that control from God, or we can yield with joy and yearning, trusting that our God is a good God, a generous God, a graceful God who always has our best interests at heart.

None of the four gospel accounts of the resurrection totally agree with one another. The number of angels, the number of disciples, the number of appearance stories — these details differ. But they all have one thing in common. They all include the enigmatic figure of Mary Magdalene, a woman whom some think was a harlot, though there is no biblical proof of that. What *is* clear is that Mary is disturbed in some way — a woman who has seven demons according to Luke.

So Mary stands for all of us who can't seem to get through a day without being disturbed in some unsettling way. What we discover, thankfully, is that God recreates Mary — God recreates us — calming us, claiming us, and yes calling us by name to become brand new. Do not hold on to me. Do not hold on to the past. Do not hold onto the fears, failures, and frustrations that have so deeply disturbed you. Do not hold onto the losses, lamentations, and limitations that have so immobilized you. Instead go! Go and tell, serve, and live. And lo, I am with you, risen and walking beside you every step of the way.

All of which suggests another central truth of Easter. For each of us who are disturbed by the problems, passions, and pressures of the past, God is calling us to the future. God is giving us a new vocation, a new purpose, a new identity, a new calling. Our new vocation is the vocation of resurrection. Our new vocation is to be God's astounding, merciful, resurrecting presence in a world badly in need of grace. Easter is as much about us as it is about God. Easter is as much about life on this side of the grave as it is about life on the other side of the grave. Easter is as much about vocation as it is about victory. Easter is when God takes our personal relationship with Jesus and cracks it open and pours it out — propelling us to love the world as much as we love God.

There are plain and practical Christians across this country who understand that our baptismal vocation as Christians is to be the embodiment of Christ's resurrection. At Central Presbyterian Church in Denver, there is a homeless shelter for men in the basement with 160 beds. It is called New Genesis and it is indeed an opportunity for disturbed people to be born again. Using a tough love approach, the men are given thirty days to change the direction of their lives with lots of help, encouragement, and counsel. Indeed, the message is clear: Do not hold onto the past but go and live as those created and re-created in the image of God. This New Genesis ministry rehabilitates and resurrects 600 men a year.

In Winston-Salem, there is a ministry called the Presbyterian Inter-Racial Dialogue — three African-American congregations and three Caucasian congregations who have done the hard work of racial reconciliation. This resurrection ministry grew out of an episode twelve years ago of racially motivated police brutality. Through racism training in the schools and the police department, through discussion groups for youth and adults, through joint worship and Habitat for Humanity projects, these faithful Christians have helped transform the racial climate in Winston-Salem. They have refused to hold onto the prejudices of the past and have embraced, with passion and purpose, God's vocation of resurrection.

So the truth of this Easter Day is that God — always mercifully and magnificently — is in charge. The truth of this Easter Day is that because the new is always more powerful than the old, we have been re-created and called to a new vocation of resurrection. The truth of this Easter Day is that all of this is possible because hope always has the final word. Resurrection is not only the vocation of our lives, but it is also the vital vision of our lives.

There is a true story that says it all. A teacher, who worked in a hospital, was sent to a little boy who was barely surviving in the burn unit. When she saw how sick he was, she felt badly about bothering him. But she proceeded to do what she had been sent to do — teach him the difference between nouns and adverbs. The next morning the nurse on the burn unit saw the teacher and asked: "What did you do to that boy yesterday?" The teacher was about to apologize, when the nurse interrupted. "We had given up on him, but ever since you visited him, he seems to be fighting back and responding to treatment."

The boy himself later explained that he too had about given up hope. But then he figured out that the school wouldn't have sent a teacher to help him learn nouns and adverbs if they thought he was going to die (Joyce Hollyday, "Wayfare," *Sojourners* 15, no. 3, 1986:19).

Hope, the most powerful truth, the most life-affirming truth of Easter. Hope — God's yes is always more powerful than our all-too-human no. My friends, as ministers of resurrection, let us go. Let us go and tell. Let us go and tell the truth of resurrection so that the world might have life and have it more abundantly.

May it be so! Amen.

Easter 2
John 20:19-30

Body Building

There is an old *New Yorker* cartoon that shows a large door, locked three times with heavy bolts. The bolts are reinforced by a sturdy chain and just to make sure that nothing can invade this formidable fortress, a long bar is securely fastened across the door post. Yet, upon close examination, it is clear that someone has managed to slip a valentine under the door.

Easter is the valentine that God slips under the locked doors of our world. No matter how hard we try to keep God's power and promise out of our lives, persistently and gracefully God reaches us anyhow. John's appearance stories begin with the disciples behind closed doors, trembling, cowering, grieving, pouting, and running away from the possibility and the promise of Easter morning. The text makes clear that the doors were locked for fear of the Jews. I wonder: What were they really afraid of? Were the disciples afraid of death or were they afraid of life — this new, strange, demanding life that a resurrected Lord might demand of them?

Now John makes it clear that Jesus "appeared" among the disciples. He didn't bother to pull back the bar or unhook the chain or painstakingly turn the three bolts on the door. Instead he just appeared. Whatever the resurrection of the body means, it doesn't mean the resurrection of the flesh. Instead it means the resurrection of the recognizable power, the recognizable love, the recognizable essence of Jesus.

Matthew, Mark, Luke, and the book of Acts all suggest that the ascension of Jesus happened forty days after Easter — followed by Pentecost ten days later. Here in John, Easter and Ascension and Pentecost all happen at the same time. The particular breath of Jesus is breathed collectively into the disciples. Why? So that as a community they might become the risen body of Christ. The resurrection of Christ is for the purpose of new creation, a re-creation *after* death, but also re-creation *before* death. It is about the creation of the Christian church, so that through the power and ministry of our life together, we might become God's continuing presence resurrecting the world. As one writer suggests, "Perhaps equating new life [only] with a life after death experience has been a way for the contemporary church to avoid our responsibility for new life now" — here in our personal lives, as well as in the life of the world (source unknown).

This wonderful picture of Jesus breathing on the disciples is reminiscent of the Genesis creation story where God breathes life into Adam and Eve. Then there is that wonderful vision in the book of Ezekiel, where the valley of dry bones all of a sudden comes alive. Breath animates the bones — they rattle, clang, dance, and rise up — coming together, covered with flesh, sinew, and muscle becoming a resurrected community of God's hopeful people. "Receive the Holy Spirit," Jesus says to the disciples locked in the upper room. "Receive the Holy Spirit," Jesus says to us, locked here in our doubt, fear, and faintheartedness. "Receive the power of life, the gift of grace, the spirit of partnership and discipleship," Jesus says, "so that you can become co-creators with me in God's world." What a gift and what a responsibility!

The passage we read from Acts this morning (Acts 2:43-47) makes clear that resurrection is experienced most powerfully in community, and it describes for us what one of the early communities looked like and felt like. It was a community of celebration, thanksgiving, awe — the poor, the widow, the immigrant, the alienated and excluded joined together with the privileged of society who had allowed themselves to be changed. They lived together, engaging in teaching, fellowship, worship, and acts of caring. With mutual love and affection, they intertwined their lives willingly and enthusiastically to embody resurrection and the scriptures attest that "day by day the Lord added to their number." Is this how the Christian church out there, the Christian church right here, is reacting to the astounding, amazing grace of Easter?

The Dutch word for resurrection is *opstanding*, which literally means to stand up, to take a stand. To be "religious," to be pious, to be holy — at least within the Christian context — does not mean to withdraw into a private world of feel good faith. It means to stand up to the powers and principalities that bring death to the world. It means to take a stand for the poor and the powerless. It means to stand up against pain, possessiveness, and pride. Yes, to be a part of the resurrected community means to be for life, not just against death.

Years ago in the *New York Times* (April 7, 1996), there was a wonderful editorial by Valerie Sayers, titled "Easter Walk." She remembers her childhood in Beaufort, South Carolina, and all the Easter fluff that went with it: pastels, silly girls in hats, new shoes, shallow schmoozing on the sidewalk following church. Sayers was a goody-two-shoes back then, very self-righteous, moralistic, and convinced that sacrifice and struggle were all that mattered in the spiritual life. She looked at the Easter parade with contempt — commercial, indulgent, silly. She much preferred the rigor and self-abnegation of Lent where she self-righteously gave up candy, butter, her pillow, and wallowed in the pain of Good Friday. She would regularly imagine herself a missionary in some far-off land, captured and tortured by the natives. Yet as a holy and pious believer, she would forgive those heathen sinners at the moment of her death. As a child, Sayers' fixation on the blood of the cross was better to her than Easter could ever be.

Then she remembers the Easter when everything changed for her. She was walking down the street with her father on a bright Easter morning in 1963 — her relaxed upbeat father who poked fun at her moralizing. Then a wealthy man came up to her father and started talking about a new private school that he was starting. Because integration was heating up, this privileged stranger was determined that his children would never mix with "those people" and watch their school sink into decline. He was confident that Sayers' father would agree.

He was wrong. Sayers' easygoing father surprised both of them by replying: "Oh, I couldn't pull the children out now. They are finally going to integrate the schools. [That] will be a great privilege for them."

In the face of death-producing prejudice and fear, this quiet, hopeful man took a stand for life. He took the good news of Easter that had just been proclaimed from the pulpit, and he turned it into practical good news for the world. Sayers remembers that moment of light and hope as the most powerful Easter of her life and throughout her life, she found herself repeating his words a thousand times: "Oh, I couldn't pull the children out now… It will be a great privilege." As, indeed, it was. These days, Sayers always buys herself a new hat for Easter — savoring butter and candy and a soft pillow. She always saunters down the street, cherishing the flowers and the sunshine, reminding herself that it is a privilege to stand up for life.

In his book *The Greek Passion*, Nikos Kazantzakis tells the story about a monk whose greatest desire was to make a pilgrimage to the Church of the Holy Sepulcher in Jerusalem, to walk around it three times and then to kneel and to pray. He was sure it would change his life and make him a better person. After years of scraping and saving, the poor monk saved thirty pounds, and he prepared to make his long hoped-for journey.

As soon as he opened the monastery door, this pilgrim was met by a beggar. The beggar asked where he was going, and the monk replied by sharing his dream and his goal: his journey to Jerusalem, walking three times around the Holy Sepulcher, kneeling and praying and becoming a better person.

The beggar responded with a very different idea. Looking at the monk with yearning in his eyes, he asked the holy man to change his plan and to give the beggar the thirty pounds for his starving family, to walk around him and kneel, and to pray that abundant life might be found for this poor family.

The monk paused for a while and searched his own heart. Then he gave the beggar the thirty pounds, walked around him three times, kneeled and prayed. He returned to the monastery a much better person. He had suddenly realized that he had seen the wounds of Christ right outside his front door in the struggle and pain of a beggar. And that resurrection, for this family, was up to him (as told by Elaine Ward, *Encountering God* [Brea, California: Educational Ministries, Inc., 1990], pp. 18-19).

Friends, as Easter people we have a choice. We can walk around the empty tomb, praying and singing and thanking God for the gift of life given to us — to me, myself, and I. Or we can go from this place, seeking the resurrected Christ in the wounds of the world. We can go from this place, standing up to the powers and principalities that bring death to this world. We can go from this place, using the resurrection power that has been breathed into this community. We can go from this place, thankfully and passionately bringing new life to God's fragile world. What will our choice be?

May it be life giving, for you and for me and for others. Amen.

Easter 3
John 21:1-19

Egg Salad Spirituality

Once in a moment of pastoral despair, Martin Luther commented on the sorry state of the human condition. He ruminated on the fact that most of us have lost the ability to shudder. We have lost the ability to feel awe, to embrace mystery, and to fall face forward at the feet of the holy.

I think that in many ways Luther is right — in our time as well as his own. Spectacular sunsets come and go but we're still too busy at the office to notice. Babies smile and crawl and explore and delight but we miss it because we're trapped on the phone or glued to the computer. Oceans roar in tempestuous wonder and caterpillars weave intricate designs but we are oblivious because we are so absorbed in our me-centered melodrama that we are blind to the wonders of nature. We listen to the astounding news of Easter morning and our rational minds recoil in dismay. My friends, we worry, we manipulate, we doubt, we conceptualize, we argue. But when was the last time we shuddered?

At the moment of his call, the prophet Isaiah shudders (Isaiah 6:1-19). This consummate temple priest is fine-tuned in the rituals of piety and worship, competently doing holy things in holy places. But it takes a while for Isaiah to experience what the holy is all about. In the process, he discovers what his life is all about. The text tells us that "in the year King Uzziah dies" Isaiah has a dream, he has a vision and it blows his mind. Out of death comes stunning life. There, high and lofty is God, filling the throne — a luxurious velvet robe covering the sanctuary floor. There is smoke, voices, and six-winged angels flying around. This polished professional priest, all of a sudden, feels awkward, overwhelmed, swept into a place he cannot control, a situation he cannot understand. "Wow! Woe!" The text tells us that Isaiah's first response is guilt, unworthiness, a sense of bewilderment. "Woe is me. I am lost. I am unclean!" (Isaiah 6:5). And yet I wonder. Is his response really guilt or is it awe? Is it really unworthiness or is it humility? Is Isaiah shying away from his own inadequacy or is he shuddering — shuddering in the midst of God's ever-alive Spirit?

There have been a few "shuddering moments" in my life, for which I am grateful. One of them occurred on July 4, 1982, at Morristown Memorial Hospital in northern New Jersey. Anna was four days old, it was early in the morning, and we were alone in our sun-drenched room. What could be more ordinary than a woman holding a baby? It turned out to be one of the most extraordinary moments of my life. Mystery washed over me, the awe of birth, of my body creating such a miracle, and of God's image being born once more in the humanity of my child. At that moment, I felt totally inadequate for the task of mothering this girl child. Yet, I also felt strangely empowered and immensely blessed to have been given the chance. On that day, in my spiritual smallness, God handed me a great and grand mission, and God gave me the grace and strength to do it. It was at that moment, I shuddered. It was a resurrection moment.

Isaiah's call is one of those wonderful paradoxes so often found in scripture. Isaiah senses his smallness in the midst of God's bigness. But this diminishing of his ego leads to an expansion and re-birth of his soul. When he understands his proper place in the vast expanse of God's grace, he becomes energized and focused on his resurrection work in God's world. It is when he shudders, surrenders, and obeys that he finds power, passion, and purpose to be a prophet in God's world. By facing the truth about who he is not, Isaiah embraces who he really is, and he hears his call to be uniquely alive in God's world.

In a similar paradox of wonder and welcome today, Jesus calls Peter and the disciples into a new and greater sense of themselves. These brash, brawny fishermen are called into the ministry of resurrection. What is most amazing about this gospel story is not that a bunch of fishermen let a carpenter tell them what to do. It is not that they forsake conventional fishing wisdom to let their nets down on the wrong side of the boat. What is most amazing about this story is the trust, the risk, the spontaneity that Peter and the disciples express. What is amazing is that Peter is willing to leave everything to follow a newly resurrected Lord, to feed unknown sheep, to go to places he has never seen, to carry out a mission he does not understand — to become the first apostle, the rock of the church. What is so amazing is that Peter starts over one more time — trusting resurrection — trusting that he can still be and become more than he ever dreamed possible.

I think it is significant that for Isaiah and Peter, the resurrection call of God comes in mid-life. Isaiah is an established temple priest holding a plum position and is settled, solid, and safe. And Peter? He has spent years honing his skills, building his muscles, learning the rhythms of the sea, and he has spent another three years following a charismatic rabbi. Both of these men have already answered several calls in their lives. As it turns out, God is not finished with them yet, just as God is not finished with us yet either. When they least expect it, and maybe when they least want it, God calls Isaiah and Peter again. God calls them to die to the old and rise to the new.

The writer, Joyce Rupp, remembers an experience that served as a sort of mid-life resurrection moment. At a crucial point in her late forties, when she was faced with making some new and radical choices, she had a dream that woke her up. In the dream she was at a party where a vast table of food was spread before her. Most of the exquisite platters held colorful, strange looking food that she did not recognize. There, in the midst of a room full of strangers, she tried to figure out which food she could eat that would be "safe." Finally she recognized some egg salad, piled it on her plate, and walked away.

When she woke up, she immediately laughed. She realized that there was no food she detested more than egg salad. Yet, in her dream, she ate it anyway because it was safe. What a revelation this dream proved to be. At that moment, Rupp realized that deeply mired in mid-life, she was afraid to leave behind the dead familiarity of her old life. She was afraid to embrace the fresh, scary, resurrection food she needed for her new life (as told by Joyce Rupp, *Dear Heart, Come Home* [New York: Crossroad Publishing Company, 1997], p. 107).

How much are we wedded to an egg salad kind of living? Are we sticking to that which is safe and familiar and predictable, nourishing ourselves with that which no longer satisfies? How much are we protecting ourselves from God's mystery, God's otherness, God's resurrection power — muffling that voice calling us to a self and a service beyond the normal, beyond the now? How might God be trying to get through to us? What is the vision or the dilemma, where is the struggle or the surprise from which God is calling to us — to rise up and go forth? Remember that it was in the midst of boredom and restlessness that God called Isaiah. It was after a frustrating night of grief and failure that God called Peter.

Then there is one more question. What is God calling us to leave behind? Is God calling us to leave the past behind? Are we like Peter? Peter had to leave all the familiar values, rhythms, and relationships — all the failures and the deaths in order to be useful in God's kingdom work. Or is God calling us to be like Isaiah who, scripture tells us, stayed put as a priest but just shifted gears focusing on prophecy instead of temple purity? Which is it? Which form of resurrection living is God calling you toward? Is God calling you to leave everything or is God calling you to rethink and reshape your energies right where you are? It's always one or the other, my friends. Life never stays the same. Our flowing, changing, growing God is always calling for us to flow, change, and grow as partners in the work of creation. God is always calling us to practice resurrection with the courage and the wonder of our lives.

May be it be so for you and for me. Amen.

Easter 4
John 10:22-30

Recognizing the Voices

There once was a great actor who was asked at a country gathering to recite the Twenty-Third Psalm. And so with great drama and flair, he mounted the stage and artfully articulated the vivid imagery of this familiar poem. The people were entertained but not moved. Later, in the same program, an old woman was asked to make some kind of contribution to the evening. She apologized explaining that she could think of nothing else to do but recite the Twenty-Third Psalm, the portion of scripture she knew best. Her voice cracked as she started "The Lord is my Shepherd." She stumbled over many of the words and the people had to strain to hear her low, uncultured voice. Yet when she was finished, there were few dry eyes in the audience. The great actor climbed up onto the stage, hugged the woman, and expressed his conviction about what had made the difference: "I know the Psalm," he said, "but she knows the shepherd" (source unknown).

Our scripture is about knowing the shepherd and the shepherd knowing us. And "knowing" has more to do with the heart than with the head. In our late twentieth-century world of agri-business, with electric fences and computerized chips keeping track of the cattle and the sheep, this scriptural image of the shepherd is a dusty antique of the past. The picture we *do* have is often romanticized and emotionally simplistic.

The countryside around Jerusalem where the post-exilic writer would have sung this psalm, and where Jesus would have painted his word picture, was dry, dangerous, and dreary. The rocky soil was a haven for hungry wolves and a trap for unsteady sheep, where steep cliffs fell precipitously to the Dead Sea below. And so, good shepherds with their staffs of comfort and rods of rescue had to be vigilant, courageous, tender, and tough.

Of greatest importance in all the confusion and danger of those rough plains, they had to intentionally work at knowing their sheep and making sure their sheep knew them. It was their voice that built the relationship. It was their voice that shaped, nurtured, and protected their flock. It was their voice that drew the lost, scared, and wounded back home. In using this homespun image to define the purpose of his life, Jesus simply says, "My sheep hear my voice, I know them and they follow me" (John 10:27).

One of the symptoms of schizophrenia, a devastating form of mental illness that breaks and confuses the human spirit, is hearing voices — loud, demanding, seducing voices that pull apart the sanity of a centered soul.

I believe in many ways that we live in a schizophrenic culture. We are bombarded with voices demanding, analyzing, projecting, pleading, persuading, seeking to control our hearts and our minds. We are a noisy, verbose culture, cluttering the air waves and the printed page with images and accusations. The only time I listen to talk shows is when I'm driving from one hospital to the next, running an errand, or driving around my geographically spread out presbytery. As one vociferous opinion follows another, I am always amazed that people have the time to listen, much less call in, to these shows — spending great amounts of time pontificating about minutiae.

The question for us today, as Christians who follow Jesus, is which and where is the voice of God? In the midst of all this noise, how do we recognize the particular tones and timbre of our shepherd, calling us to the purposeful safety of spiritual wholeness? How do we sift through the voices in our heads and our hearts, listening to the one voice that matters, so that we can become centered in wholeness, and we can defend ourselves from the splintering tongues of cultural and personal demons?

If we consider the Twenty-Third Psalm with fresh eyes and attentive ears, we may hear some new nuances of meaning. The verbs alone help us to understand how God works and what God says in our lives. The presence, the voice of the shepherd leads, comforts, restores, anoints, prepares and sometimes, when we are recalcitrant and stubborn, makes us rest. These are all images of nurturing, empowering, encouraging — giving to us the freedom and responsibility to grow, stretch, and move toward wholeness. The shepherd does not drag us, deplete us, bombard us, accuse us, or violate us in order to get his way or force us into his image. Instead, the shepherd's voice invites, waits, and walks by our side. And in the life of a diverse and growing flock, there are three places where the voice is the strongest.

The first place is beside still waters where the sheep are made to lie down in green pastures. It is interesting that this is the first and not the last place we hear the shepherd's voice. Rest and restoration of the soul is not the last place the shepherd leads us, but the place where our growth and our creativity begin. As the writer of Revelation makes clear, these still waters are also living waters, the place where God's Spirit can fill us and sustain us for the journey of life ahead. Yet, how often do we respond to the pushing, demanding, driving, judging voices in our lives first, failing to hear or listen for God's still small voice, inviting us to rest and restoration, to solitude and centering?

There is an ancient story coming from the desert fathers. When a novice would first enter the monastery, the abbot would ask the seeker to bring with him a bowl of water from the desert. Putting the bowl on the ground, the novice and the abbot would sit and watch, until all the sediment had settled on the bottom, and the water became clear. Then the abbot would explain. "Your life used to be like that murky water. But now, as you enter the silence with God, your heart can become clear and open. Then you will be better able to reflect God, who can best be seen and heard by the pure in heart."

The voice of God is that voice, amidst all the hectic noise, which urges us, leads us, and sometimes with physical manifestations, makes us lie down to rest in green pastures beside the still waters.

But that is never where we stay, for the voice of the shepherd also leads us to right paths, to paths of righteousness, and to straight paths that take us home. With all the rocks, caves, and wolves luring the sheep in dangerous directions, it is only the familiar voice of the shepherd that can redirect them — redirect us — toward home and toward physical safety, moral righteousness, and spiritual wholeness.

A few years ago, there was an interview on NPR with Eduard Shevardnadze, the former Soviet bureaucrat, who had emerged as a compassionate and tireless shepherd of the struggling Russian Republic of Georgia. He talked about the strong convictions he once held as a Communist, his certainty in a rigid and ideological way that the tenets of Marx and Stalin were the appropriate voice for the peoples of Northern Europe. But when he became the head of the Communist Party in the Republic of Georgia at the height of the Soviet empire, he learned the hard way that communism just doesn't work. The corruption, the rigidity, the heartless vision of undemocratic socialism did not touch the needs, unleash the creativity, or celebrate the spirit of the Georgian people. So, he became instrumental in resisting and ultimately destroying the communist empire.

After Perestroika, he felt called back to Georgia to lead it on the straight path, the right path, the path toward freedom and democracy. He found his work as the shepherd of a fragile flock difficult, dangerous, and discouraging. But he did not give up, because he himself had heard the voice of the good shepherd leading him, restoring him, and anointing him with purpose. At the age of 67, Shevardnadze was baptized, literally throwing off the old and robing himself in the new, immersing himself in the living waters of Christianity and attuning his ear to the only voice that could lead him and his people, on paths of righteousness toward freedom, and toward home.

We know that we are hearing the voice of God when we find ourselves resting by still waters and when we feel ourselves moving on straight paths of righteousness. There is one more place where we hear the shepherd's voice — the place we need that voice the most — and that is in the valley of the shadow, the valley of evil, the valley where hurt, despair, and death threaten to overcome us. In the scripture lesson from Revelation, the risen Christ gathers all the tribes together to celebrate the wholeness and peace promised when God's work is finally done. Yet, all those happy, free people have been through the great tribulation — an imagined time of terror, violence, and destruction — and in the great paradox of faithful living, the white purity of their robes has only been obtained through the blood and sacrifice of suffering.

In the mid 1990s, during the televised memorial service for the victims of the Oklahoma bombing, Billy Graham spoke of the tenacious presence of God in the valleys of the shadows of our living. He said that though there is no answer to the question "Why? Why did all those innocent people die in such a violent, evil way?" There is an answer to the question "Where? Where was God?" God was with them in the valley of evil. In his simple way, Graham summarized the rich comfort of religious faith when he said, "I'd rather suffer with God, than without God."

We can be sure that God is with us in the valley and that the voice will always be able to sustain, rescue, and heal us because God has been there. The shepherd has been the lamb, slain and maimed by the violent and unpredictable forces of evil and pain. And that experience as the lamb so changed and shaped God, as the shepherd, God will never ever again forsake the sheep. God knows, God understands, God feels the terror of the valley. As the apostle tells us, we can be absolutely convinced that God will never leave us there, and God will come back into the valley, finding us, calling us, and carrying us home.

My friends, amidst all the voices, there is a voice making us to lie down by still waters, leading us with vision on paths of righteousness, walking with us in the darkest valleys of our living. But we must listen, learn, and follow. That is our hope and that is our calling.

May it be so for you and for me. Amen.

Easter 5
John 13:31-35

Love's Integrity

One day I was walking Maggie in a meadow of wildflowers near our home. It was early evening and the simple beauty of it all was feeding my soul. But then Oliver interrupted my reverie. Oliver is a white lab and he was frolicking on the other side of the meadow — that is until Maggie saw him and tried to take off. Maggie loves other dogs and wants to make intimate acquaintance with any canine cousin who might cross our path. So Oliver and Maggie connected with each other and began to bark and sniff and thoroughly enjoy each other's company. That left me to talk with Oliver's mistress, a woman from Russia, who was visiting some friends in our neighborhood. After introductions, this woman reached out — with great joy and delight — to touch the cross that I was wearing. "What religion are you?" she asked. I responded that I was Presbyterian, which engendered a totally blank look from my new friend. I quickly simplified my answer to say that I was Christian to which she responded with a broad grin. "Ah, we are alike," she said with an accent as unlike mine as one could imagine. She then told me that she was a Russian Orthodox and enthusiastically explained how wonderful things are now for Christians in Russia. We talked a few more minutes and then I dragged Maggie away.

That simple encounter has stuck with me over the years. We were total strangers from opposite ends of the earth but after just a few minutes, I felt more connected to this woman than most people I see on a given day. By acknowledging each other as Christians, we all of a sudden realized how much we had in common: values, images, stories that set as apart from the confused and fragmented chaos of the secular world. By unabashedly touching my cross with its arms open in universal inclusive love, this stranger made me feel loved and accepted, and I felt the same about her. Together we are the body of Christ and individually members of it. And that identity stands as a sign and a promise of what this world can be like.

Our scripture lesson this morning set the standard that defines this universal body called the church and that literally sets the church of Jesus Christ apart from the world. You see, the church, at its best, provides what Walter Brueggemann calls "an alternative consciousness" among the peoples of the earth. In what might be seen as a rather arrogant statement, our old Presbyterian Book of Order states that: "The church of Jesus Christ is the provisional demonstration of what God intends for all of humanity" (G—3.0200). That implies *what* we, as Christians, say and do and *how* we say and do it is crucial. Our witness is the yeast in the loaf, the light in the darkness, the sign of hope and healing in a dark, troubled, abused, and abusing world.

Jesus names for us today how this "set apart identity" is shaped and nurtured. He offers a "new commandment" which, at first glance, seems neither "new" nor very "commandment"-like. His words come at a transitional point in the gospel of John — at the end of his public ministry, and before the agony and beauty of his passion. They are the introductory words to the final discourse, a three chapter farewell speech that Jesus gives to his disciples in order to prepare them for his death, and to bless them with the promises and challenges of their future. The setting of this passage is the Last Supper, immediately following the washing of the disciples' feet.

Now, as most of us probably recall, the synoptic gospels — Matthew, Mark, Luke — have Jesus offering *two* "great commandments" directed not only at the intimate bands of disciples but also to the crowds. "You shall love the Lord your God with all your heart, and with all your soul, and with all your strength, and all your mind; and your neighbor as your yourself" (Luke 10:27). In John, however, the two commandments are collapsed into one, and they are addressed only to the disciples, set apart from the world, in that upper room. And rather than commanding them to love their neighbor as themselves, Jesus says, "Love one another, as I have loved you" (v. 34). A very different focus than the other gospels.

This is "family talk" intended not for everyone, but for a committed, intimate group. It is not that the gospel of John ignores the world. Instead what Jesus is saying through the perspective of John is this: "You who claim to be disciples of mine, I commission you, I plead with you, I command you to love one another in a unique way — to love one another with a sensitive, understanding, tolerant, inclusive love — to shape and model a diverse community that can demonstrate to the world what God intends for all of humanity. It will only be when you together become my resurrected body in physical form, empowered by my living spirit — it is only then that the world will be able to continue to encounter me, to encounter God in human flesh."

Jesus anticipates their resistance and their sense of inadequacy. "What do you mean, Lord? How do we do it, Lord?" It is then that Jesus invites them to love one another *as he has loved them*. To love one another as he loved Nicodemus, meeting the Pharisee where he was, taking seriously his intellectual doubts, gently leading him from a judgmental legalism to spiritual flexibility. To love one another as he, Jesus, loved the Samaritan woman at the well — overcoming the prejudices at that ancient world, by honoring the humanity of a foreigner, breaking custom to speak to a woman in public and gently confronting her with her broken life and then inviting her toward wholeness. Loving one another as he, Jesus, loved the woman caught in adultery, accepting her and forgiving her unconditionally, condemning those who reject her because of her lifestyle and inviting her to new life. Loving one another as he, Jesus, has just loved them, honoring them and serving them with physical humility, as he has done by washing their feet. Yes, Jesus makes it clear what it means for Christians to love one another when he points to his own example. To love one another means to take ourselves out of the center and put the needs and good of the whole community first, to become a unified plurality woven together by love, which *is* the presence of God in community.

The companion scripture lesson, which is assigned, for this Fifth Sunday of Easter, is the story of Peter and Cornelius in the book of Acts — a fairly new addition by the ecumenical lectionary committee. Much to the dismay of his traditional friends, Peter, a devout Jew, has eaten and defiled himself in the home of a Gentile, thus breaking the purity laws of the Jewish tradition. In times past, Peter, himself, has been adverse to reaching out to someone whose history and lifestyle he did not understand, but in a dream — the most familiar way God speaks in scripture — Peter is told "to make no distinction" and to overcome his fear and his dis-ease, and accept and include Cornelius in his life and in his previously closed community. "Love one another," Jesus says, "as I have loved you."

Martin Buber, the great Jewish philosopher who worked at the beginning of the twentieth century, gives us a clear sense of what this love — this *agape* — is about. Buber suggests that the most helpful human relationships are "I-Thou" relationships where each person acknowledges the divine image in the other and acknowledges that the other person is precious and human. Unfortunately, most of our relationships tend to be "I-I" relationships, where the other is seen as like ourselves, thus denying that person's uniqueness. Or

"I-it" relationships, where the other person becomes an object we use for our own benefit. Or "I-Them" relationships, where we allow the other person's different-ness to turn him into an automatic enemy. Now, Buber does acknowledge that there are also "I-You" relationships, where the other is affirmed as human but no intimate or spiritual connection is made. He readily admits that this is the quality of most of our interactions in the daily public realm. But using Buber's typology, "I-Thou" relationships — the ones that demand intentional commitment, humility, other-centered intimacy, and open-mindedness — this kind of covenant relationship is at the heart of the love that Jesus calls Christians to live out.

There is a story told by a newly arrived mission worker in Africa. She was assigned to be the chaplain in a leper hospital, one of the most miserable places on earth. Because all the patients were lepers and thus highly contagious, they were socially marginalized. Very few visitors ever came to break the monotony. There was one man in particular who emotionally touched the young chaplain. He was a former village leader, who had lost all his power and privilege in the world, and had become very bitter. Every day he would lie on his back in the dirt, unable to move because of his decayed and amputated legs. Whenever the missionary would come close and try to speak with him, he growled and turned away. Finally one day, the young chaplain bent down and placed herself on the ground next to the man. They both lay there in silence, the sun scorching their skin. Finally, the old leper asked: "What are you doing?" The young woman responded: "I thought it might be good if I saw the world from your point of view." That simple gift of love changed the man's life. From then on he welcomed her visits and her prayers, and his bitterness began to transform into possibility. "Love one another as I have loved you." Empathy and solidarity with suffering is at the heart of the love that Jesus calls us to share.

Jesus calls his disciples — he calls us — to love one another in a unique way, a way that sets us apart from the world. He calls us to love one another with a love that encourages souls to touch and to love one another with a love that considers the strengths and weaknesses, the needs and dreams of each member. In this corporate, communal love we present an alternative vision to a world centered in self, to a world splintered by individualism. It is this love, creating us together into the resurrected body of Christ that allows the world to continue to encounter the reality of Jesus. It is into this body that we baptize and are baptized, and it is discovering and living this love that becomes the meaning of our lives. My friends, this is the gift and the invitation of the Christian faith.

May it be so, for you and for me. Amen.

Easter 6
John 14:23-29

The Present Tense of God

When I decided to preach on this text, I was excited about the hope, the energy, and the promise of Jesus' words. But this week, when it came time to decide what to say, I found myself decidedly less enthusiastic. Quite frankly, when I reread these words from John about peace, untroubled hearts, and the comfort of the Holy Spirit, I found myself saying "You've got to be kidding!" I don't know about you, but when I look around at our battered, belligerent world, peace is the last thing I feel.

As a nation we have been shattered by terrorism and unsettled by economic decline. As a congregation we have lost too many wonderful people in too short a time from illnesses that were too brutal and painful. The scandal of child abuse in the Roman Catholic church, echoed by the many cases of clergy misconduct in the Protestant church, turns our stomachs. Most unsettling for me in this particular time in which we live is what is happening in the Middle East.

I have hesitated to say anything from the pulpit about the mess in God's Holy Land for several reasons. The situation is so volatile that what I say today may be irrelevant by tomorrow. Having visited and traveled in the West Bank years ago, my own feelings run very deep. So my outrage often colors my thinking in intolerant ways. In this place, where we share sacred space with our Jewish brothers and sisters, we are at a particularly delicate crossroads in our continuing relationship with the Bethesda Jewish congregation. As deep as my friendship and respect is for Rabbi Sunny Schnitzer, and my other Bethesda Jewish congregation friends, I do not trust myself to talk with them about what is happening in Gaza and the West Bank, for the stand-off in Palestine and Israel is happening in the birth place of God's embodied shalom — the birth place of the peacemaker Jesus — the one whom we know as our risen Lord and Savior.

If Jesus were here today, what would he say or do about the past decades in the Middle East? What would he say about 23 Jews being slaughtered by a suicide bomber as they celebrated the joy and freedom of Passover? What would Jesus say about the killing of a Palestinian friend's landlord? This father of five was ordered by Israeli soldiers to drive to George's building in order to unlock an apartment they wanted to search. The landlord obeyed only to be murdered by the same soldiers — 22 bullets pumped into his head. Why? Because he broke the curfew that forbids Palestinians to be in the streets — the very same streets he was ordered to drive through! What would Jesus say about Israeli generals who call Palestinians "lice" and a "cancer" upon the earth? Or about the Palestinian leaders who call Israeli soldiers "Nazis"? What would Jesus say about Arab young adults so embittered and disempowered that they blow themselves up along with dozens of innocent civilians somehow considering this "holy work"? What would Jesus say about Israeli tanks obliterating buildings, destroying schools, building massive security walls, refusing to allow doctors to treat bleeding and dying people, preventing women in labor from getting to a hospital — all in the name of security?

If the good news of the gospel is meant for all times and all places, what is the good news of the gospel for the Jews, the Muslims, and the Christians of the Middle East? What is the good news for us, immobilized and helpless in our anger and our confusion? If we can figure out what Jesus would say and do, then maybe we can figure out what we might say and do, for as the body of Christ alive in the world today, Jesus' message can only be delivered through us.

These words from the final discourse Jesus offers this morning give a clue. They are spoken less than 24 hours before his own brutal murder on Golgotha — a death brought about by the power politics and religious wrangling of his own day. Sitting amid the remnants of the Passover meal, the remnants of the freedom meal, Jesus gives his disciples a gift. He gives them the promise that despite the death and the blood, the terror and the division, they will not be left comfortless. They will not be left orphaned. He promises that he, Jesus, is leaving them a legacy — a legacy of peace — a legacy of shalom. But, Jesus says, this is not a peace like the world thinks of peace. It is not simplistic, chauvinistic peace, based on security and self-interest. No the "peace" Jesus lives and leaves is a peace that is rich, complex, and cosmic. It is a vision of a harmonized creation where all of God's creatures can experience abundance, justice, and grace.

So, Jesus' promise is not primarily about personal peace. It is about communal peace, and it describes a *way* — a way of being and a way of becoming. It is the same "way" that has taught, healed, loved, and transformed the disciples while Jesus was been in their midst. This way, this peace, is a gift he is leaving for the whole world. Not just for the disciples but also for the Jews and the Gentiles, the Greeks and the Arabs, for the whole host of humanity who are *all* God's people.

So, we must ask: Where is this peace? Where is this way and truth and life that Jesus promises to leave us? Where is it in today's tumultuous world? It is wherever men and women cherish this vision of shalom — this vision of justice, respect, compassion, and harmony for all God's people. It is wherever we are able to submit our personal agendas to the cleansing and shaping of a global agenda. This vision is wherever we are willing to say that what is healthy and hopeful for me must be helpful and hopeful for you — whether you are like me or not.

In terms of the Middle East, the peace Jesus leaves and gives, is embedded in whatever proposal offers land and security, justice and abundance to all the people living in that region. Peace means to figure out a way to share Jerusalem — as a witness to the world that our common God speaks Hebrew and Arabic, English and Latin — and this global God loves each language and each peoples the same. Peace means those few Israeli soldiers who have refused to fire upon innocent civilians or bulldoze schools and homes. Peace means the pleas of a Palestinian father grieving over the body of his child — pleas calling not for retribution, but for peace — for the end of such senseless killing. Peace means interfaith statements issued by the religious leaders of Jerusalem and a plea for an immediate cease fire signed by a representative of Israel's Chief Rabbinical Council; by the deputy foreign minister of Israel; by the main religious official of the Palestinian Authority; by the Orthodox, Armenian, and Latin Patriarchs; by the Anglican Bishop of Jerusalem. Peace means Christians, Muslims, and Jews re-writing common school curriculums, taking out the language of hate and enmity and replacing it with visions of hope and harmony. Peace means ordinary American Christians praying daily with passion and hope — praying that peace *will* be victorious. Peace means the modest witness of two suburban congregations — one Jewish and one Christian — speaking truth to one another, sharing sacred space, confronting stereotypes and prejudices — one small window into how peace and shalom can be embodied and how very different people can honor a common God.

In saying farewell to his disciples, Jesus does not just leave a legacy of peace. He also promises a way that this legacy can continue to live and can continue to live and move and have its being. Jesus promises a Spirit, a Holy Spirit, an advocate, a counselor, a comforter who will come to be the living power of God in their lives and in our lives. He promises the "present tense of God" (phrase from Michael Lindvall) now and forever.

As Trinitarians, those who profess faith in a God who is Father, Son, and Holy Spirit, we are bold to proclaim that God is present, here, right now — present in our midst, here in our lives, here in our world, here in our hearts, in our wills, in our minds, and in our bodies. Like water rushing in to fill every nook and cranny of the ocean, so is God a permeating presence, a persuasive presence, a nourishing presence available to us now — in us and for us — empowering *us* to be peace for the world. (Thanks to Marjorie Hewitt Suchocki for this image.) So, we *do* have the resources to be peacemakers, to be global shapers, to be together hope and harmony for a world of shalom. Each of us can, and must, figure out something we can do and something we can be to honor Christ's legacy of peace.

In the early 1970s, Nobel Peace Prize laureate Betty Williams first woke up to the cauldron of hatred threatening to obliterate Northern Ireland. She witnessed the bombing death of Irish children — helpless victims in the rage-filled conflict between Protestants and Catholics. A little girl died in Williams' arms, her legs severed, after having been thrown across the street by the explosion. Williams went home in shock and despair. Later that night, unable to sleep, the reality of what she had experienced jolted her into action. She stepped outside her door, screaming in the middle of the night. She knocked on doors — both Protestant and Catholic — that might easily have opened with weapons aimed at her face. At each house she cried out: "What kind of people have we become that we would allow children to be killed on our streets?" Within four hours the city was awake and there were 16,000 signatures on petitions for peace — the beginning of a peace process that thirty years later finally bore fruit (as told by Frederic and Mary Ann

Brussat, *Spiritual Literacy: Reading the Sacred in Everyday Life* [New York: Scribner], p. 356).

My friends that voice of outrage, that voice of compassion, that voice of hope was the voice of the Holy Spirit, the advocate, filling the aching cavern of Betty Williams' heart. It was a voice of peace — of shalom — of possibility for an unfinished world. This day let us open our hearts to the power of the Holy Spirit. Let us allow that Spirit to fill the aching void of our hearts with a vision of peace. Let us become the present tense of God — voices of outrage, compassion, and hope for our still unfinished world.

May it be so. Amen.

Ascension of Our Lord
Luke 24:44-53

The Promise

A friend tells of her visit to her 95-year-old grandmother in Ohio. Grandma has been Teri's mentor and soul mate for 45 years. But this time Grandma did not recognize her favorite granddaughter. Teri writes about the visit: As we sat talking about the insignificant stuff you talk about with people you don't really know, I laid my hand on her back. She immediately leaned forward and as I started rubbing her back she began smiling and purring. When it was time to go, she asked me to come again soon. The next day when I arrived at her door she looked up and smiled. "Good morning, Grandma," I said. "Do you remember me today?" "Of course I do," she replied indignantly. "You are the girl who rubs my back" (as told by Teri Thomas).

Touch. Touching the reality. Touching the fragility, the woundedness of old age. Touching what is instead of what used to be. Affirming life even in the threatening shroud of death. It was a holy moment for Teri and for her grandma.

This morning it is touch, touching the reality of woundedness, which becomes the proof of resurrection. It is followed by a promise, the promise of power that precedes Christ's ascension, power for the work of resurrection. We are still hearing resurrection stories six weeks after Easter. Because Easter is not a day. Easter is not a season. Easter is the relentless, renewing promise of the Christian life. Every day we are pushed, shaped, and "threatened by resurrection" — by God's tenacious touch — leading us through our woundedness toward wholeness.

The scene from the gospel of Luke sounds eerily like the gospel of John — one of the few places that the "human" gospel and the "mystical" gospel intersect. It is several days after the first resurrection encounter on the road to Emmaus and now Jesus is "all of a sudden" standing among the disciples. No one — even Jesus himself — knows how he got there. But there he stands: wounded, scarred, alive — he stands among them and declares, "Peace be with you. Wholeness, promise, harmony, justice be with you." The disciples are terrified so sure that they are seeing a ghost.

Now this terror is interesting, because Luke has just told us that they have already seen the resurrected Jesus once. They have seen him and then recognized him in the breaking of the bread. So why are they startled now? Why are they scared now? Why are they incredulous this second time around? Is the "ghost" the vision of a living Jesus? Or is the "ghost" the urgent vision, the urgent call of peace, this declaration that personal and social peace is both possible and present?

Whenever Jesus talks about peace in the gospels, he is talking about shalom — that vision rooted in the prophetic writings of the Hebrew scriptures. Peace, for Jesus, is not some warm fuzzy, personal serenity. Peace for Jesus is robust, complicated, and harmonious community. Though peace is initiated by the Holy Spirit, it only becomes reality through us.

The prophet Micah gives us a glimpse of peace in this corporate, more complicated sense of shalom. Writing at the time of the exile, when the contentious, faithless people of Israel have been dragged into captivity, Micah encourages them with a vision of the future — a future when God will forgive and restore Israel. The picture Micah paints is glorious. It is of people streaming to God's mountain from all the nations. Men, women, and children walking in God's path, instead of following their own treacherous detour. Swords, guns, and bombs beaten into ploughshares, the end of war and violence, the end of hatred and intolerance, this is the end of prejudice, greed, and selfishness. A time when all people will have a tree and a vine to call their own. A time when no one will ever be afraid again.

What a vision! What a vision for ancient Israel! What a vision for the terrified, listless disciples in Jerusalem! What a vision for the people of God right now. As this vision shimmers like a ghost in our midst this day, do we see it? Do we believe it? Or like those disciples are we startled? Terrified? Filled with doubt?

Jesus addresses the doubts of the disciples — disciples back then and disciples today — in a very concrete way. He shows us in graphic detail his wounds and he asks us to touch. He rubs our noses, our hearts, our senses in the bloody reality of his pain and death — in the bloody reality of treachery and suffering. Jesus does this to remind us that resurrection only comes after crucifixion and that shalom shimmers even after death shatters. Until we touch the wounds — feel the pain and smell the death of a broken world — we cannot receive the ascension promise, the promise that we will be given power from on high, power to transform a violent world into a resurrected world.

So let us look, let us see, let us touch, let us abide in Jesus' modern wounds for just a while this morning. Let us contemplate the work of resurrection that the ascended Lord leaves in our shaky hands. Imagine in your mind the extended belly of a four-year-old girl in the barren sand of Ethiopia. She is but one of the two thirds of the world's children who are threatened by death from hunger and malnutrition. How could this wounded picture change if we Americans spent less money on dieting and more money on alleviating hunger?

Imagine in your mind eight children suddenly reeling, falling, bleeding at the entrance to the zoo — part of the reality of firearm injuries which is the second leading cause of death among teenagers in this nation. As the columnist Colbert King reminds us, the same kind of gang and turf tension existed in the 1950s amidst the teenagers in Washington DC but homicides and injuries were much less. Why? Because parental values were more intact and handguns were not readily available. How could this wounded picture change if strict licensing of handguns became a reality in this nation?

Imagine in your mind the broken body of Greg Barnes hanging by a noose in his garage — a scholar/athlete at Columbine High School haunted by the shooting of his favorite teacher before his very eyes, haunted not by the gracious ghost of peace but by the ghastly ghost of violence, haunted so malevolently that he was led to hang himself.

Brothers and sisters, the risen Christ is showing us his wounds this morning in the extended belly of the that four-year-old girl, in the bleeding bodies of those eight Washington children, in the broken neck of Greg Barnes. Christ is offending us with his wounds. Why? So that he can transform us with his will and bless us on our resurrected way.

We know, of course, that Jesus' wounds are not the end of the story. Beyond woundedness, beyond crucifixion, beyond injustice and hunger and violence and revenge, is resurrection — a vision of shalom planted deep in the soul of every human creature. It is that vision Jesus blesses us with before he ascends — a blessing that leaves us to be his witnesses and his resurrected body on earth. It is that shimmering shalom that draws us beyond the now and beyond what is real today toward what is possible tomorrow. Jesus does not leave the disciples with his wounds. He leaves the disciples with his promise, his promise that possibility and peace will come upon them and that they, and we, will be clothed with power from on high — power to transform shadows into shalom — power to transform woundedness into wholeness.

I am part of a community of clergy that meets twice a year in the home setting of one of the group members. Most recently, the Pastor's Community met in Santa Fe, New Mexico, to meet the living Christ in the rich colors of our nation's high desert. One afternoon we heard from a gentle, young father who works at Los Alamos, the epicenter of American nuclear power. A physicist by training, James Doyle is a classified scientist at Los Alamos and an elder at the First Presbyterian Church of Santa Fe.

He surprised us by indicating that 25% of the employees at Los Alamos are working as peacemakers — working on the non-proliferation and reduction of nuclear weapons. Jim's particular work is focused on helping the devastated economy of Russia eliminate the nuclear weapons industry and transform a weapons economy into a technological economy. Being the meddling type that clergy tend to be, one of our group asked Jim what his Los Alamos work has to do with his faith. He thought a minute and then said that he feels like David, approaching the Goliath of violence with the slingshot of peace, but he is convinced that David can win. He believes that the current philosophy of deterrence — just build bigger, more expensive weapons in order to deter the violence of the enemy — is basically absurd. Deterrence is based on the premise that killing and destroying is the best that we as divine creations think we can do. Deterrence dehumanizes the enemy and accommodates to human imperfection, thus denying the transforming power of God's presence and promise.

Jim went on to paint for us a hopeful vision, the kind of witness to resurrection that the disciples are called to in this gospel text. This vision is real for Jim because he trusts in something beyond human wisdom and human resolve. He trusts that he, and we, have received the "power from on high." Jim believes that in his lifetime we will see a reduction to a total of 500 nuclear weapons worldwide — vastly different than the 50,000 nuclear weapons that currently exist. In his vision, those 500 weapons will be under the control of the United Nations or some other international body. The only way any one of these nuclear weapons could ever be used would be after unanimous consent of all the partners in this international coalition — a destructive decision very unlikely if global well-being is considered ahead of national well-being. Is this vision naive? Perhaps. Desirable? Absolutely. Attainable? Only if we trust that the "ghost" of resurrection is the reality of a risen and ascended Christ, wounded but whole, living, breathing, and continuing to recreate us in our very midst.

On this Sunday in Eastertide, we are wedged between the promise of resurrection and the work of resurrection. But the power is coming in a couple of weeks — the power of Pentecost, the power from on high, re-creating us one more time and equipping us for this work of resurrection. The power can only come upon us after Jesus has been lifted up, after the earthly Christ becomes the ascended Christ, after the particular Christ becomes the cosmic Christ and available in all times and in all places.

We are being called to wonder — to touch and proclaim that the "ghost" of resurrection is real. Then we are called to wait and to trust. To wait to be clothed with power from on high and to trust that the promise of peace will become the presence of peace as we embody that peace in our lives.

This is the good news of the gospel. May it be so for you and for me. Amen.

Easter 7
John 17:20-26

Rubbed Raw Love

Our larger denominational family, the Presbyterian Church, USA, is currently giving new meaning to the phrase "dysfunctional." Like most historic mainstream Protestant churches, we Presbyterians are shrinking at alarming rates. Now, small or at least smaller is not always a bad thing and in fact, it is a very biblical thing to be — but only if we are passionately living out the gospel message. From my perch as a governing body leader, what has shrunk more than anything else in our mainstream, Protestant psyche, is our commitment, our fervor, and our understanding of the good news. In many places, we have lost the conviction that through our baptism, the Spirit of a living Christ gives us the power and the call to change the world, to transform greed into grace, cruelty into kindness, despair into hope, and the brokenness of the world into the wholeness of the world. As a cradle Presbyterian — a third-generation Presbyterian pastor — my grief about the changing world of the Presbyterian Church, USA, is not our diminished membership. My grief is about our diminished faithfulness.

Now some folks will tell you that the reason the Christian witness in America is fading is because of the debates we have had through the years about supposedly "political issues," proclamations opposing particular wars; a thirty-year struggle to open the offices of the church to gay and lesbian pastors, elders, and deacons; strong statements about the environment, immigration, nuclear armaments, Middle East politics, capital punishment, and restorative justice for prisoners — some will say that we have caused our own demise by focusing on controversy instead of the peace and joy of God's love. Except folks, our entire biblical story gives us a lot more to think about than peace and joy.

Cain murders Abel, Jacob wrestles with Esau for his father's blessing, Aaron sabotages Moses, James and John argue about who is the greatest, Peter and Paul disagree about circumcision and kosher food, in Corinth the rich and the poor bicker about who should eat first, the Galatians disagree about who is saved, and the Romans have the first argument on record about the proper separation of church and state. As one blogger has written:

> *Sometimes I think we expect God to be present only in the clean parts of life. We talk about God's presence when things go well... but in Genesis God is present in... sibling rivalry and reconciliation, the founding and the falling of nations, the failures of the faithful as well as their triumphs. God is present in the messiness and the monumental — the mundane and the magnificent. Perhaps we should look for God even in the messiness of our own lives.* (Dan Ott)

Our gospel text is a powerful witness to the inevitability of conflict among believers. It is also our Lord's final and most fervent prayer on behalf of his disciples. The feet of the disciples are still wet from the touch and cleansing of servant Jesus. Outside, in the inky night, Judas is collaborating with the Roman soldiers, setting up the arrest and eventual death of Jesus. These final hours of Jesus' life are filled with ferment, division, and violence. Yet it is the midst of such foreboding and brokenness that Jesus begs God to unite the disciples and to keep them connected with the kind of intimacy, trust, and blessing that unites Jesus and God. Such a connection is not a gentle bond, but a fierce bond, a kind of unity that cannot be broken by betrayal, debate, doubt, or despair. And with quiet passion, this prayer also becomes Jesus' most fervent dream for the church.

However, unity does not mean the absence of tension. Scott Peck, the psychiatrist and bestselling author, once wrote an essay about marriage. He reflects on his own thirty-year covenant with his Chinese-born wife and he makes it clear that harmony has never been the secret to their long life together. In fact, he claims that the only reason for any of us to get married is what he calls the "friction" — the creative energy that differences, arguments, and power struggles inevitably unleash. Peck concludes that the true test of married love is not the times of romance, but the times of conflict. Why? Because it is during tough times that the only way forward is to submit ego and self to the greater vision of the whole — to put the "we" before the "me." Then, Peck says, we need to be prepared to be changed in the process.

Friction is inevitable in any family and particularly within the family called the church. In a metaphorical sense, every congregational struggle is akin to Esau and Jacob wrestling for the power and blessing of God. And God, it seems, is always purposely present in the struggle.

In the 1980s I served a small parish in New Jersey. The major conflict in that congregation turned out to be new curtains in the fellowship hall. This sounds minor, but believe me, it was major! The older women wanted to replace the old curtains with the same thing: drab, heavy, lined drapes that had to be dry-cleaned. The younger women, on the other hand, wanted to rip down those dowdy, dusty window coverings and replace them with bright floral curtains made out of permanent press bedsheets. This controversy simply spun out of control until I called all the women together, sat them down, and then locked the door. I informed them that until we had this issue settled, none of us was leaving. Well, they fussed and fumed and then talked things out and finally the floral bedsheets won the day. Why? Because they were cheaper and the younger women volunteered to do all the work! Thus began years of collaboration and friendship that wove these two antagonistic generations of women together and strengthened the entire church. Creative "friction," indeed!

Then there were the arguments that we endured as the body of Christ in the congregation I served in Maryland for seventeen years. Some of the issues we struggled with were significant: funding fancy musicians versus increased mission outreach in the community, whether or not to keep our wonderful associate pastor when he came out of the closet as a gay man, the push back when the session made a prophetic statement opposing the first Gulf War, whether or not to build new common space with the Jewish congregation that had shared our sacred space for over 35 years… well you get the point. Every Christian community I have ever been part of in my 62 years of living has confronted the fact that we are all sinners, and that our churches are inevitably full of people who disagree with each other. The challenge has always been to show to the world that Christians can deal with differences and conflicts in healthy and productive ways to demonstrate to the world how Christians can be one despite our diversity and differences. Some may ask why should we even bother "playing nice"? It is because the creation of unity amidst diversity is in the very spiritual DNA that soaks into our souls when we are blessed by the waters of Christian baptism. It is Jesus' most fervent dream for the church.

I believe differences are what build a strong, creative, and diverse congregation — a unity not based on uniformity, but on the submission of each person to a vision and calling bigger than any one of us. As Paul writes in Galatians (ch. 5), the fruits of the Spirit are *not* "enmity, strife, jealousy, anger, quarrels, dissension or factions." Instead, the fruits of the Spirit are "love, joy, peace, patience, kindness, generosity, faithfulness, gentleness, and self-control" — all values that are absolutely necessary if we are to answer Jesus' final prayer — "that we might all be one." Such hard-fought harmony does not come easily, and it demands that everyone give up part of their vision and power so that the whole body can live, breathe, and grow in God's grace. It is this kind of commitment that is necessary and creates what writer Kathleen Norris calls the "sufficient unity, the rubbed raw, but sufficient love" that makes room for all God's people to belong to the body.

For 2,000 years, those of us created and called by God to shape the world in the image of Jesus Christ have struggled to become community, to be more together than any of us can be alone. It is sinful human nature to believe that we are right and that others are wrong. But the truth is that God uses each one of us and in the end, God also blesses each one of us for one reason and one reason only. We are blessed, my friends, in order to become a blessing to the world.

May it be so. Amen.

If You Like This Book...

Susan Andrews also wrote "The Offense of Grace" for the Advent/Christmas/Epiphany section for **Sermons on the Gospel Readings**, Series I, Cycle A (978-0-7880-2323-1) book $36.95, e-book $29.50.

Other Cycle C Lent/Easter Lectionary Titles...

Living Vertically
John Brittain
978-0-7880-1731-5
printed book $12.95 / e-book $8.95

Deformed, Disfigured, and Despised
Carlyle F. Stewart III
978-0-7880-1716-2
printed book $12.95 / e-book $8.95

contact CSS Publishing Company, Inc.
www.csspub.com **800-241-4056**

Prices are subject to change without notice.

Taking the Risk Out of Dying
Lee Griess
978-0-7880-1030-9
printed book $13.95 / e-book $8.95

Living the Easter Faith
Donald Dotterer
978-1-55673-522-6
printed book $12.95 / e-book $9.95

CPSIA information can be obtained at www.ICGtesting.com
Printed in the USA
LVOW101430090612

285330LV00005B/11/P